Transition to Freedom
Fearless Woman – Part Two

Foreword by
Dr. Christopher C. Gee

Pearly Gates Publishing LLC, Houston, Texas

Transition to Freedom
Fearless Woman – Part Two

Copyright © 2016
J'Anmetra "Jo-Jo" Waddell

All Rights Reserved.
No portion of this publication may be reproduced, stored in any electronic system, or transmitted in any form or by any means (electronic, mechanical, photocopy, recording, or otherwise) without written permission from the publisher. Brief quotations may be used in literary reviews.

Unless otherwise stated, Scripture references are taken from the King James Version of the Holy Bible.

ISBN 13: 978-1945117084
ISBN 10: 1945117087
Library of Congress Control Number: 2016939499

For information and bulk ordering, contact:
Pearly Gates Publishing LLC
Angela R. Edwards, CEO
P.O. Box 62287
Houston, TX 77205
BestSeller@PearlyGatesPublishing.com

WHAT OTHERS ARE SAYING

"*Fearless Woman* is an autobiography written by J'Anmetra Waddell detailing her life with her abusive husband, Pastor "Jamal". In her words, "In public, Jamal was an amazing man! At home, he would spend the entire day spewing out the following words: You're ugly. You're stupid. You will never be anything. You're a nobody. You had better be glad I married you; no one else wants you but me."

"The book navigated readers through J'Anmetra's tumultuous journey – one filled with countless daunting days leading up to her victorious escape. *Fearless Woman* reveals the horrifying truths of emotional, psychological, and financial abuse that exists in conjunction with physical abuse.

"*Fearless Woman* is a powerful source of encouragement that will empower anyone facing abusive defeat and will help them find their voice."

Benita K. Brunson, M. Ed.
Adult Education Mathematic Teacher

"It's really a defining experience in a person's life to write a book – especially one as personal as J'Anmetra Waddell's Fearless Woman: Born to Give Thanks. The book is an inspirational memoir about overcoming the effects of life's trials, ups and downs, and pains and joys caused by circumstances of life. That amazing book exemplified months of euphoria, solitude, struggle, despair, and hope. Becoming a writer takes courage. Fearless Woman is a testimony of J'Anmetra's courage.

"I admire Ms. Waddell for accounting the intimate details of her journey with candid honesty. The book chronicles her faith in God to bring her to the place of blessings and prosperity for her family. Her journey ends in victory and a life beyond hardship. Through her perseverance, there is the "overcoming" that brings blessings and prosperity from God and the test of faith in one's self to live on in spite of the obstacles."

Much Love,
Elder Jennifer Jennings
MBA, HR Consultant

"Inspirational and transparent is what first comes to mind when I think about J'Anmetra Waddell's *Fearless Woman: Born to Give Thanks*. It was a story that needed to be told. I felt every word. It was hard to swallow knowing that those things could happen to anyone – especially a Pastor's Wife. Silent pain. I felt her pain. This is riveted. I didn't want to keep reading, but I could not stop. I had to know what happened next.

"The woman I met is not the woman who went through what happened on the pages of *Fearless Woman*. Or is she? See, we don't know the next woman's story. J'Anmetra made it so you felt her story. You were walking in her shoes.

"I'm looking forward to the next installment of her story. Thank you, J'Anmetra, for sharing your story. Many women are going to be healed and set free because of it."

Katherine Waddell, CEO
This Needs to Be Said Media, Inc.

Amazing Grace!

"Fearless Woman: Born to Give Thanks was submitted for consideration for a book award for The Writers' Ball 2016. Once the reviewing committee completed their recommendation, I picked up the book, began reading it, and did not know what to expect. I could not put it down! I was so consumed with what I was reading. You see, I first thought it was a fictional piece written by an accomplished author. After reading several chapters, I looked back over the first few chapters of the book, referred back to the title, read the submission report, and realized I was reading a true story by an emerging author.

"This beautiful author went through Hell at the hands of someone she loved…her husband. I hurt for her while reading her unbelievable – yet true – story. How could a human treat another human like that? Still, Ms. Waddell wears her crown so beautifully that you would have never known she experienced a living Hell – and probably death had she not trusted GOD to get her out of that situation.

"*Fearless Woman* is a must-read for anyone who is going through domestic violence or knows/suspects someone who may be experiencing something similar. Many did not have the courage to get out of their violent situation. Many tried to leave, but were unsuccessful. Many died at the hands of the men they loved and trusted. Thankfully, this author lived to tell her story."

Sha Battle, Founder/President/CEO
The Writer's Ball
Dance with the Stars Atlanta
Kidz Rock! Awards
Black Women's History Month

"*Fearless Woman: Born to Give Thanks*. A powerful non-fiction story that will uplift, educate, and motivate those who have found themselves in a subtle domestic abusive relationship.

"Through one woman's journey to escape the mental bondage of fear, Author J'Anmetra Waddell takes us with her as she unfolds the hurtful truth of being an emotionally-, physically-, and mentally-abused Preacher's Wife."

Veronica Coney
Healthy Inspirational Living Coach

Dedications

Transition to Freedom is dedicated to every woman who is starting over. It doesn't matter where you are starting over from…all that matters is that you decided **TODAY** is the day you start anew.

We are born to be great! Do not spend your life conforming to who your family, friends, or the world wants you to be. You will miss the opportunity to reach your full potential simply because you have not liberated yourself from the constraints of the world.

~ *J'Anmetra L. Waddell* ~

Acknowledgments

To my girls: You are beautiful. I desperately want your foundation to be strong. You girls are the reason why I work hard, never stop, and oftentimes never sleep. I want to give you the foundation you need so that when you are ready to jump and spread your wings, you have a great base under your feet. Thank you for giving me your unadulterated advice – although oftentimes unsolicited. I appreciate your wisdom and vision that you openly share. I love you beyond measure!

To my friends who "keep me in line and focused" *(you know who you are)* by giving me the full and unadulterated truth of my reality: I cherish you more than you may ever know.

Again, to Angela Edwards and Pearly Gates Publishing: Our journey has been amazing! Thank you for walking it with me. God is doing amazing things through you, and it is my honor to be a part of it.

Thank you to everyone who has provided an encouraging word, prayer, and support. I love you, I appreciate you, and I am amazed that you chose me to be in your life.

Preface

"It is so liberating finding the essences of who you are."
~ J'Anmetra L. Waddell ~

Writing *Transition to Freedom* – the continuation of *Fearless Woman: Born to Give Thanks* – was more difficult than I thought it would be. I often found myself being pulled back into that dark space of the early years.

I relived the fear.

I relived the nightmares.

I relived the sweats, the racing thoughts, and the self-doubt.

On numerous occasions, I found myself staring at the box of memories I had not opened in over 10 years. Within the box were letters from Jamal, notes written to myself, the research I had completed, and court papers that documented the terrors of my past life. I read words I thought I had finally gotten over and moved past. I cried new tears. I cried new frustrations and relief. In the midst of it all, I began another healing process – one I had no idea I desperately needed.

As for you, Dear Reader, I pray that as you read my story, you come to realize that the major point of *Transition to Freedom* is to take one second, one minute, one hour, and one day at a time. You don't have to have all the answers right now. You **WON'T** have all the answers right now…and that is okay. Accomplish what you can – one day at a time.

I desire for you to understand that as you begin to love yourself again, *breathe*. What do I mean by 'breathe'? When we are stressed, we tend to (oftentimes unknowingly) hold our breath. Doing so removes the ability for us to think and see clearly. Doing so stifles our understanding and prevents us from functioning in our purpose.

In that moment, **STOP** and **BREATHE**.

Your body will respond.

You will realize that at least for that moment in time, as long as you **BREATHE**, everything is going to be okay.

Foreword

Fear is the resultant answer to acts or impending acts of terror that have high probability of causing harm or further harm. Fear can leave a person in a state of mental or physical paralysis. It can be gripping…squeezing the very precious sense of hope out of one's being. It commits thievery…stealthily robbing its victim of sound reason. It is demoralizing…weakening the morale to levels of severely diminished self-worth.

What does one do when faced with such a daunting entity?

Author J'Anmetra "Jo-Jo" Waddell is a living testimony of the maleficent power and influence of fear. In her riveting first book, *Fearless Woman: Born to Give Thanks*, she painstakingly detailed her experience of being consumed by fear; but rather than accept her dire situation as her final reality, she stared the chimera of fear in the face and, with a penetrating gaze, acted in defiance to better her reality. What an awesome display of courage in spite of the probable repercussions! With the fervor of determination, J'Anmetra escaped the bondage of fear and reclaimed her destiny.

In this book, *Transition to Freedom*, J'Anmetra promises to take the reader across an unforgettable trek of intriguing terrain as she reveals with vivid details the continuation of her deliverance from the abysmal life riddled with abuse and how she segued into the blissful reality of freedom.

Prepare your *mind* to learn from this incredible woman.

Prepare your *heart* to be moved with compassion.

Prepare your *soul* to be encouraged through her experience.

Dr. Christopher C. Gee
FHIR Works, Inc.
Mount Holly, North Carolina

Introduction

Being **FEARLESS** all began when I decided to share my story with the world. It was not an easy decision. Some days, being **FEARLESS** took (and sometimes *still* takes) all the courage that I have. However, being **FEARLESS** is the only way I want to live my life!

We spend our entire lives being what the world wants us to be; not who we were *created* to be. We were born to be great! Still, some of us may never recognize our full potential simply because we are not bold enough to liberate ourselves from the images that the world, our family, friends, and even the workplace have impressed upon us.

Never be apologetic for your path in life! *Never* apologize for the leader, the writer, the singer, the dancer, or the inventor in you! It is okay for other people to be uncomfortable with who you are. It is not **your** responsibility for them to accept you!

At the age of 40, I instantly understood that I had to quit being who I was and start being who I was born to be:

A LEADER.

A TEACHER.

A TRAINER.

A THOUGHT-CREATOR.

A REBEL!

I welcome you to come with me on this journey of being **FEARLESS**! Together, we can change the world…one **FEARLESS** person at a time!

Table of Contents

WHAT OTHERS ARE SAYING 6

DEDICATIONS 12

ACKNOWLEDGMENTS 13

PREFACE 14

FOREWORD 16

INTRODUCTION 18

EXCERPT FROM *FEARLESS WOMAN: BORN TO GIVE THANKS* 23

CHAPTER FORTY-ONE 23

CHAPTER FORTY-TWO 24

CHAPTER FORTY-THREE 25

CHAPTER FORTY-FOUR 26

CHAPTER FORTY-FIVE 28

CHAPTER FORTY-SIX 31

CHAPTER FORTY-SEVEN 32

CHAPTER FORTY-EIGHT 33

CHAPTER FORTY-NINE 34

CHAPTER FIFTY 36

CHAPTER FIFTY-ONE 38

CHAPTER FIFTY-TWO 40

CHAPTER FIFTY-THREE 41

CHAPTER FIFTY-FOUR 43

CHAPTER FIFTY-FIVE 45

CHAPTER FIFTY-SIX 48

CHAPTER FIFTY-SEVEN 49

CHAPTER FIFTY-EIGHT 50

CHAPTER FIFTY-NINE 52

CHAPTER SIXTY 54

CHAPTER SIXTY-ONE 57

CHAPTER SIXTY-TWO 59

CHAPTER SIXTY-THREE 62

CHAPTER SIXTY-FOUR 65

CHAPTER SIXTY-FIVE 68

CHAPTER SIXTY-SIX 71

CHAPTER SIXTY-SEVEN 74

CHAPTER SIXTY-EIGHT 76

CHAPTER SIXTY-NINE 78

CHAPTER SEVENTY 79

CHAPTER SEVENTY-ONE 82

CHAPTER SEVENTY-TWO 84

CHAPTER SEVENTY-THREE 87

CHAPTER SEVENTY-FOUR 88

CHAPTER SEVENTY-FIVE 95

CHAPTER SEVENTY-SIX 96

CHAPTER SEVENTY-SEVEN 97

CHAPTER SEVENTY-EIGHT 99

CHAPTER SEVENTY-NINE 101

COMING SOON 103

ABOUT THE AUTHOR 104

APPENDIX 106

Excerpt from *Fearless Woman: Born to Give Thanks*

CHAPTER FORTY-ONE

One day, I looked through the phone book for an 800-number help-line. I needed help. I knew I couldn't just walk away from Jamal: I needed someone to come and get me!

I remember getting up one morning and going downstairs to the den. I crouched behind the recliner and dialed the 1-800 Domestic Violence Hotline and asked the lady only two questions before I hung up:

1. *Could she protect me from him?* and
2. *What did I need to do?*

CHAPTER FORTY-TWO

Jamal didn't call what he did 'cheating'. He often denied looking at pornography. When I asked him about it, he eventually stopped responding to my questions. He called the online-dating that he was doing while we were married as him "doing research for a new mother for his child". He didn't want me to raise her because, as he said, I wasn't a good mother or role model. He wanted to find someone to take my place who I could train before he killed me – so that my youngest daughter would grow up to believe 'that woman' was her mother.

CHAPTER FORTY-THREE

I became a professional makeup artist from the many instances of covering up black eyes and bruises around my neck and on my face. I wore sunglasses year around – even in the winter months when it grew dark before it was time to pick up my daughter. The daycare providers never asked me about what they saw, but I could still see the look of pity on their faces – even with the sunglasses on. A few of them did ask, *"Why the sunglasses?"* I would reply with some off-hand answer, but none of them reached out to me to ask if I was okay.

CHAPTER FORTY-FOUR

Our baby stayed in the hospital for 31 days after her birth. When we went to visit her, the nurses would try to get her to breastfeed. That enraged Jamal. On the way home, he would scream at me for allowing the nurse to try to force the baby to take my nipple. He said, *"If she wanted it, she would take it."*

He didn't care that breast milk was what was best for her – especially after being born premature. After a couple of unsuccessful tries, I was instructed to tell the nurse we would be using the bottle. That allowed him to feed her while not allowing for me to get attached to her.

After all, I wouldn't be around long enough for any of that to matter.

My life **was** on the line…daily.

The *Transition to Freedom Begins…*

CHAPTER FORTY-FIVE

The sun was shining, but it provided no warmth for me. I was shaking most of the time. I kept looking for Jamal to show up anywhere and everywhere to kill me. I knew it didn't matter to him if he killed me in public or private – as long as I was **D.E.A.D.** That was always his promise to me: If I ever left him and took the kids, he would never stop looking for me. He would hunt me down and kill me.

The day I left Jamal for good was filled with crazy things. Thank goodness my friend was thinking for me because I was on robot-mode. She had me change my address to hers so that I could receive my unemployment check. She made sure I had clothes by taking me to a local consignment shop and telling them I was going through. They gave me a $100.00 voucher for clothing. It is a humbling experience to have to buy second-hand underwear, bras, and everything. Even the small things you take for granted that are no longer at your fingertips – like a toothbrush, comb, diapers, milk, and money - were a blessing. I offered to volunteer for them. It was the **least** I could do to repay them for giving me the necessities just to feel human again.

Jamal called my friend's house the day after I left and said that he was extremely concerned about the girls and me. He told her he loved me very much and only wanted to make sure we were taken care of – especially because the baby was a preemie and was in need of a specific type of milk. He went on to explain that the baby was delicate and needed to be taken care of.

After about two hours on the phone with Jamal, my friend ended the call. She was upset and crying. He had told her that I was following her and treating her as if she was my God. He chastised and accused her of teaching me to hate him and to not go back to him. I actually felt sorry for her because she wasn't used to his ramblings like I was. For me, what he said was simply his everyday – and normal – chatter.

I went to the bank the next day to withdraw some money out of the account because my unemployment check had been deposited. When I arrived, the teller said, *"Ms. Jamal, this account has been closed."* I told her, *"That's impossible! My unemployment check is direct-deposited into it!"* She replied, *"No, ma'am. It's not. Mr. Jamal closed this bank account on yesterday."* He cleaned out the checking and savings accounts (*not that there was much in there*). I **still** have the envelope with my notes from that day and the printout of when he closed the account.

I guess he wasn't worried **too** much about his daughter having milk and diapers…the three diapers I had taken when we left were long gone.

While staying at my friend's house, she let my children and me have her son's room. There was a TV in there. I was so conditioned on what I could and could not watch, I didn't even turn on the TV for the first couple of days. When I did finally turn it on, the first movie I saw was *Drumline*. I sat there in a daze and watched. I know, I know. It was a movie that had no meaning – at least in the beginning – yet there I sat, hypnotized by it. *Drumline* was the first black movie I had seen in two years. Jamal didn't like watching black movies. He said it stereotyped black men and women, so we were not allowed to watch anything that had black actors in it.

Drumline became my favorite movie. It symbolized my first step of defiance. I watched what I wanted to watch…**AND** it was a black movie! It was a very tiny step towards making a decision all on my own, but it was mine – and I *LOVED* it! The movie still makes me giggle every time I watch it.

CHAPTER FORTY-SIX

My first week without Jamal was the longest week of my life. I was staying with a friend he didn't know. He had no idea who she was nor where she lived. For the most part, I felt as safe as I was ever going to be.

Most of my days were spent staring out the window and looking at my baby. When she cried, I cried with her. I functioned as best I knew how when it came to caring for her. I provided her with the most basic of fundamentals: clean diapers and regular feedings. The connection a mother and child should have was nonexistent. I desired to have it…to establish it…but I didn't know how.

I **forced** myself to hold her.

I **forced** myself to talk to her.

I **forced** myself to tell her that I loved her.

CHAPTER FORTY-SEVEN

While at my friend's house, I phoned my mother to tell her I had left Jamal. I can't say that I recall her response, but I do remember telling her where I was. She then sent my sister to pick me up.

I returned to my other friend's house – the former church member who I remained friends with – and waited for my sister to pick me up from there to take me to my mother's house.

I remember feeling so nervous. I was worried about how I looked in the clothes I was wearing. By this time in my life, most of my apparel was a little too big. I felt unkempt, nasty, dirty, embarrassed, ugly…and that I was the worst parent ever.

When my sister arrived and walked through the door, I was on the phone with my mother who was checking to see if my sister had arrived. My mother made me hug my sister (*she's not the touchy-feely type at all, so the hug was not fully reciprocated*). As soon as our embrace ended, she turned to the baby and immediately started crying. When she held her, she cried even harder. For the next three-and-a-half hours, she cried nonstop and refused to put the baby down. From that day forth, the baby has been "my sister's baby".

CHAPTER FORTY-EIGHT

When I first saw my mother, we hugged each other tightly. Her embrace was full of love – and she even told me as much. Strange thing: My family has never been big on saying "I love you". Thinking back on it, I believe that was *the first time* I can remember my mother saying out loud that she loved me.

Since that moment, we say it **every** single time we hang up the phone or part ways. I'm sure it's because we realize how precious time truly is…

CHAPTER FORTY-NINE

In order to have Jamal keep his distance from me, I had to have charges pressed against him. My friend took me to the courthouse – and I was a nervous **wreck**.

As I walked through the courthouse doors, I was shaking and could barely utter a word. I felt the room go dark. *Was I sitting or standing?* I wasn't sure. My skin was both hot **and** cold.

I didn't want to see Jamal ever again, so how was I going to stand in front of and testify against him? Everywhere I looked, I thought I saw him. I tried to stay close to as many officers as I could or stay mixed in with large crowds of people. Believe it or not, I was still uncertain whether or not I wanted to press charges against him. I was worried that his ministry would suffer, that people would think he was crazy, that they wouldn't believe me, and that he would never be able to get a job. I had a fleeting thought: *"Who am I to do this to this man?"*

Maybe I **was** the crazy one. Maybe all the things he said about me were true. Think about it: *I did just leave a home and my husband for a shelter where I was wearing other people's clothes – and I had two children in tow.* One of the two children was a preemie who had only been home for a couple of months. I was without **any** means of caring for them…or me. *Who was I to insist the court system protect me? Who was I to make the choice to leave the man who professed to love me?*

CHAPTER FIFTY

I recall the difficulties of finding a job right after the baby was born and released to come home. It was truly difficult because Jamal insisted that I take the kids with me to fill out applications and go on job interviews.

I was so embarrassed when one agency told me, *"Ma'am, you cannot bring a newborn with you on a job interview."* What other choice did I have? He had given me a timeframe in which to get a job because the rule of the house was this: I was to work. It was Jamal's job to focus on his ministry while I provided the income for the home.

There were always rules.

The rules for going out of the house included:

1. *Do not speak to your oldest child. You are her mother, not her friend. Do not touch her.*

2. *Do not let the oldest child touch the youngest child. She wasn't good enough to be around the baby, so that included not being permitted to touch her.*

3. *Come straight home. No detours. No talking to anyone. No looking at men.*

After job-hunting for a couple of hours, the baby was hungry. Since I was driving, I had the oldest feed her a bottle. When we returned home, Jamal asked the oldest what we did. She responded, *"Mama let me feed the baby."*

Well, after sending the oldest off to bed for the night, the remainder was spent with he and I in the den with him reminding me why she is not allowed to touch the baby. I remember standing in the den by the wall. I was holding the baby at the time. Jamal took my head and pushed it into the brick wall. He caught the baby just before I dropped her. Before crumbling to the floor, I remember him yelling, ***"I don't want to tell you again: She is not allowed to touch the baby!"***

CHAPTER FIFTY-ONE

The days (yes, **DAYS**) I went to the courthouse to process the paperwork was a chore. The stress from going through was pushing me to quit. At one point, I considered dropping the charges and going off to hide out from the world for the rest of my life!

The following account of my experience is **no** exaggeration:

Every single time I completed a form and returned it for filing within the court system, the woman at the desk would tell me, *"You need another form. You have to go to floor such-and-such to get it."* This process went on for a few days before every step had been completed.

Oftentimes, I wanted to go around that counter and sit on the lady. She stood about four feet tall and had to step up on a stepping stool to get to her chair at the counter to assist the customers. It would have been easy to take out my frustration with the system on her…

Nothing – and I do mean **NOT A THING** – was easy as it related to completing the paperwork process. Once I was done at the courthouse, I then had to take it to the Sheriff's Deputy's Office for it to be processed. The female Deputy who was to issue the subpoena to Jamal instructing him to appear in court stood at about six feet tall and had beautiful dark skin and dark hair that was pinned up. Next to me, she looked like a giant!

I told her I was afraid that Jamal was going to come and find me to kill the kids and me. She told me not to worry about that because she was a Sheriff's Deputy – a big Black woman with a gun – and he was not going to hit **her**! Of course I was thinking, *"You're crazy, too! He is going to kill you as soon as you try to serve him those papers!"*

The police promised to take care of me after Jamal was issued the subpoena to appear in court. They told me I had to show back up to court two weeks later to testify against him.

CHAPTER FIFTY-TWO

Waiting those two weeks for the court date to arrive was beyond difficult. The days were long and the nights endless.

In the interim, I tried my best to learn how to take care of my baby. At times, I was almost afraid to even *touch* her. I didn't know how to make her stop crying. I could not nurse her. The darkness and depression of just **looking** at her sometimes was overwhelming. All I could think about were all the things Jamal told me…that she was going to grow up with a lousy mother.

Thankfully, the friend who took my daughters and me in also had an infant (*our daughters were two months apart*). She was able to provide things for my daughter that, at the time, I was unable to afford or emotionally provide.

Most days, it was all I could do to get out of bed, take the kids to school, and return home. One night before bed, my oldest asked if we could pray for Jamal. She went on to say that even though he was a bad person, she was *sure* God still loved him. I absolutely did not want to pray for him, but when a 7-year-old says something like that, you oblige. So, we got on our knees and we prayed – *although (**admittedly**) my prayer in the beginning was filled with hate, anger, frustration, madness, bitterness…and tears.*

CHAPTER FIFTY-THREE

As mentioned previously, there was a consignment shop that blessed me with a $100 voucher for clothing. On that day, I told the owner, *"If you ever need a volunteer or other support, I am more than happy to help."*

(I reemphasize: I don't think I can put into words what it was like to wear used underwear and bras. I cannot express the shame that hid behind my eyes as I avoided eye contact due to the pitiful nature of my situation.)

The following morning, I received a call from the consignment shop. They said they needed me to volunteer. After meeting the woman I was to assist, we began talking and I shared a bit about the circumstances that brought me to them. She recommended a program that was for people who had been previously incarcerated and couldn't find a job (*that wasn't my situation, but it was a lead nonetheless*). Her friend happened to be the Director of the program. She phoned her friend, told her a bit about me and my situation, and they allowed me to attend the one-week training.

In the training, they provided clothes for interviews, completed your resume, and worked with companies who helped those with 'troubled' backgrounds.

In the beginning, I was so judgmental of those in the program. After all, I wasn't a criminal. (*Little did I know...that would eventually change.*) However, by the end of the program, I had made plenty of friends and walked away with a job at IBM.

For the first time in a **VERY** long time, I felt like I was moving in the right direction.

CHAPTER FIFTY-FOUR

The day I was to appear in court, I was so sick to my stomach. I was vomiting and had diarrhea. I was paranoid and having anxiety attacks. I couldn't stop shaking. I started to hyperventilate. All of this was going on…and I was all alone. My friend had to go to work, and there was no one else available to take me to court.

I remember walking through the security station at the courthouse. All the while, I was thinking, *"How was Jamal going to get a gun or knife through this to kill me?"* Unfortunately, that thought gave me absolutely no sense of security whatsoever.

I was having difficulty locating the courtroom I was scheduled to appear in, but I remembered where the office was of the Deputy who served Jamal the papers. I walked to her office and busted out in tears. I couldn't find the strength to tell her what was wrong, but she stopped everything to pray for me. After that prayer, I calmed down.

Did I fail to mention that the Deputy was a minister in the same denomination…and that she happened to know Jamal? When she told me this, I just knew she was going to find him, bring him to me, and force me to go back with him.

She escorted me to the courtroom. As she did, I was leaning heavily on her while we were walking. I'm pretty sure she was holding me completely up. To this day, I have no idea how I made it there (*Did I float on air?*), how I entered the courtroom (*Did I simply become a ghost and become one with the door?*), or how I made it to my seat (*Did the Deputy carry me?*). I do recall my legs feeling like they were made out of Jell-O. I felt like I was in a tunnel. I was there in body, but my mind was nowhere to be found.

In my mind, I imagined how Jamal was going to kill me. He would run into the courtroom with guns blazing and shoot me down. I envisioned my children learning about the murder on the news. I could almost hear the 5:00 p.m. reporter's familiar voice sharing the **Breaking News** during the afternoon soap opera *All My Children* or *One Life to Live*:

> "*J'Anmetra Waddell was killed today by an angry spouse while attending court proceedings…*"

CHAPTER FIFTY-FIVE

While sitting in the courtroom, I thought about everything Jamal had **ever** said to me. I thought about how wrong I was to be there pressing charges against him.

I would destroy his ministry and all that he had built.

He wouldn't have a job or a way to support himself.

I would destroy his character.

I would be putting all of his business in the streets.

Time and time again, I thought, *"I shouldn't be doing this"* ... but yet, there I was!

The Deputy sat with me as long as she could until she was called away. Again, I was left alone. I tried as best I could to sit close to the officer in the courtroom without being in his lap. Every time the door to the courtroom opened, I was too afraid to look back to see if it was Jamal entering. The one advocate who was assigned to the Domestic Violence Court was too busy with the other women to focus exclusively on me. I needed someone just for me. I didn't want to share her. I wanted her to hold my hand and tell me she was going to protect me. I needed security. Unfortunately for me, the advocate couldn't provide it.

I was convinced he was going to tell the courts I was crazy which would, in turn, get me locked up and I would lose custody of my children. After all, didn't he try that before?

When the judge finally entered, it seemed to take forever to get to my case. One after another, I heard every woman's story. Oddly enough, they **ALL** sounded eerily similar to my own.

When my name was called, I was too scared to move. Another Deputy helped me walk to the seat beside the judge. The judge asked me why I was there and to tell him what happened. Suddenly, I had no voice. Words would not exit my mouth. I thought I was choking and then I started to cry again. I remember the judge leaning in close and telling me, *"It's ok. I'm going to help you and make sure Jamal never hurts you again."* In response, I shook my head. The judge allowed me to whisper the answers to his questions in his ear. He immediately granted me a Restraining Order for one year.

I can't say I felt *good* about being granted the Restraining Order, but I did feel **better**.

Jamal never showed up to court that day. I did, however, check all of my surroundings when I exited the courthouse. The walk to my car was like walking from the Earth to the Moon. I felt as if Jamal was in every car and every shadow was him.

CHAPTER FIFTY-SIX

When Jamal and our little family first moved to Raleigh, we visited a shelter and hired the help of some of the men there to help us unload the U-Haul into our storage unit. Jamal and I picked up three men, took them to the unit, and instructed them on what to unload. While the men were working, Jamal told me to get back in the car. He then accusingly asked me, *"Do you want to screw those men?"* I said, *"What are you talking about?"* He proceeded to explain:

"You took your jacket off in the car and acted like you wanted their attention. Is that what you want, you whore? Is it?"

I had no idea what to think or say. That was only the second time he had ever said **anything** like that to me. Honestly, I was too scared and shocked to respond.

After my obvious denial to reply, he said, *"Just admit it – and I will forgive you."*

I would come to learn that admitting anything – even when it was a lie – would be the answer for **everything**. As long as I admitted to doing whatever **he** thought was wrong, he would forgive me…and teach me how to love him the correct way.

CHAPTER FIFTY-SEVEN

I never take for granted being able to ride in my car with the windows down. The wind blows through, the smell of the air tickles my nose, and the feel of the warmth of the sun on my skin is divine. Moments like that make me want to giggle and laugh out loud and lures me to visit the park and sit on a swing.

I oftentimes find myself looking into cars that are passing by. When I see a woman and man in the car and the woman isn't smiling, I immediately wonder: *Is she sad? Is she crying inside? Is she a victim of abuse? Is she – like I used to do – staring out the window wishing someone would stop the car and save her?*

One of Jamal's pet peeves was me looking into other cars as they passed by **– especially** if there was a man in the car. When I was with him, I often stared out of the car window and wondered what it would be like to drive with the windows down – and without his cigarette smoke clogging up the interior and attaching its awful smell to my clothing…

CHAPTER FIFTY-EIGHT

One of the local women's shelters offered free counseling. I decided to take advantage of the opportunity. I went once a week to meet with the counselor. She allowed me to talk as much as I wanted to. Meanwhile, my oldest daughter talked with another counselor. Speaking with the counselor helped the most because it allowed me to sort my thoughts out.

These are just **SOME** of my transitory thoughts:

- *I had no idea who I was.*
- *I had no idea what I was doing.*
- *I had no idea why I was doing it.*
- *I had no idea where I was going.*
- *I had no idea why I was going.*
- *I had no idea in Hell on how to get to wherever it was I was supposed to be.*
- *I didn't know which direction to turn, what to say, how to say it, how to be…I didn't know anything.*
- *I didn't know* **ME**.

I knew my name and that I was a mother of two girls, but I had no idea who I was. I often looked in the mirror and just stared at myself. Even that was hard in the beginning after first leaving Jamal. When I looked in the mirror, all I heard was his voice:

"Look at you! You're fat! You're ugly! Your hair is too short to be a First Lady! You don't carry yourself like a woman! No one is going to love you! You're nasty! You're a whore! You're a prostitute! You're not a good mother! Those kids are going to turn out to be horrible if they live with you!"

CHAPTER FIFTY-NINE

I stayed with my friend – the former church member – for three months. During this time, I found a job and was happily and gainfully employed. The car was working the best I could afford to keep it running. When that third month came, it was time for me to find my own space and figure myself out.

I was driving through a neighborhood one day (*well, actually, I was lost*) and saw a house for rent. After a little negotiating with the owner, I had a new place to live! At the time, I had nothing but clothes to my name. I had **no** bed, **no** couch, **no** TV, **no** *nothing*; just the used clothes acquired over the course of the past three months.

Getting that house was the first time I could remember genuinely smiling about something in far too long...

The house was in a quiet neighborhood where 100% of my neighbors were retired. My family came through for me and provided a bed for me. The Director of the volunteer program gave me a royal purple couch out of her living room and an old floor-model TV.

My nights were long and sleepless. Some of the habits I developed when I was with Jamal kicked into overdrive. My nightly routine – without fail – was to put the girls to bed then check all the windows in the house to make sure they were locked. I would double-check the doors and double-locks. Then, I would unlock the front door, step outside, and look up and down the street to see if I saw his car. I would go back inside, lock the door, recheck the windows, check on the girls, and sit on the couch to watch TV for **exactly** 10 minutes. When those 10 minutes were up, I would repeat the entire process. I did that every single night for *months*.

When I was finally able to find sleep, the nightmares came. My bedroom window was high up on the wall, so the car lights that came down the street would make strange shadowy shapes. When I would wake from a nightmare, it felt like Jamal was standing over me trying to choke the life out of me. Other times, I envisioned him with a knife in his hand or standing in my closet staring at me. I often thought I heard his voice in my ear. When I had those nightmares, I would get up (*keeping the lights out*), and repeat the nightly ritual: check the windows and doors, step outside, look for him, come back inside, check on the girls, watch TV for exactly 10 minutes, and start all over again...on the hunt for a peaceful night's rest.

CHAPTER SIXTY

The new job was working out great! I was up at 5:00 a.m. to get the kids ready to drive them the 30 minutes to school and then another 30 minutes to work – then do it all in reverse at the end of my shift.

The first couple of years were beyond rough. Gas money was few and far between. Often, money was nonexistent – and so was food. I would often eat lunch at work and not eat again until the next day, just so my children could eat. I found myself picking up any change I found on the ground. After all, pennies turn into dollars! Trust me; they came in handy.

I found a store in town called "From Jesus with Love". It was a discount store of sorts that sold food and clothing. The cost to get in was $3.00, and you could take only the things you could carry out. The first time I went, I had three one-dollar bills. Without fail, no matter when one would go, there would be a line wrapped around the corner. (They only let a few people in at a time.) Once I entered, I was guided to a small area with a few chairs. The attendant read a passage of scripture, spoke a few encouraging words, and asked if there was anything she could pray for. After prayer, I was free to continue into the store. *Again: I could only take what I could carry.*

My **first** time there, I found it difficult to carry anything with my baby in a carrier and a 7-year-old by my side. Still, I left there with enough food for the week. A majority of the time, meals consisted of egg noodles, vegetables, or potatoes. I became an expert at making up recipes. For example, I would drain the juice from the vegetables, add them to the egg noodles, and sprinkle parmesan cheese on top. **TA-DA!** Dinner! If it was potatoes, I would bake them and serve veggies on the side. Meat became a luxury, while vegetables, beans, and potatoes became main meals.

It was time to put my creativity to the test. I didn't take me long to figure out how to **best** capture the blessings of the "From Jesus with Love" store with the $3.00 in pennies I had collected from the ground during the week: I would have empty backpacks on the front and back sides of me. My oldest daughter would have two backpacks as well. The baby would be in a stroller – not in her carrier.

I would load up the stroller with clothes (*I became a master at rolling the clothing very small and then would tuck them around the baby and under the stroller to get as much as I could*). I had to work fast because the facility put a time limit on how long each shopper could stay.

For the food section, I would have my oldest put the canned goods in my back backpack. Everything else would go in my front. For her backpacks, I would put the fresh vegetables, diapers, and milk (*if they had it available*). The fresh bread would be carried in our hands.

I left there knowing that my shopping trip would last us a couple of weeks when I portioned it correctly.

Some days, I would pull up to the house and have my oldest stay in car while I went inside to see if the lights were still on. I didn't have the money to pay the electric bill, and there were only so many times I could go to the agencies for assistance. I would pray all the way home for the lights to still be on. If the lights were on, I would go outside and get the girls out of the car. If they weren't on, I would call my friend and she would let me stay with her until I got paid again and could pay the bill to restore service.

I also became a professional at knowing how far my car could go on 'empty'. I knew that if the gas light came on while on my way to work, I could make it home and back to work the next day before I **absolutely** had to have gas money. That meant I had a full day to find money for gas to get back to work.

CHAPTER SIXTY-ONE

I was able to find a great school for my oldest daughter. They were strict and had a system in place for learning that I loved. After meeting with the principals – who happened to be husband and wife – my daughter was set for school.

One of the helpers in the classroom was looking for extra income, so the principal introduced us. The helper ended up watching my daughters while I worked. (The woman was Muslim. I soon learned the mosque she attended distributed boxes of food for $2.00 every Tuesday. The box of food consisted of chicken, breads, and vegetables. Between them and the discount store, that was how we survived.)

My salary of $12.29 an hour didn't go very far after rent, lights, gas, insurance – and no public assistance. I became even more creative with mealtimes. Chicken and fish were cheaper when bought in bulk, so I would purchase, divide it up, and freeze it. *Did I mention meat was a treat?*

The girls' favorite meal became the egg noodles and vegetable juice concoction I made. Rice was often a staple, too. With the leftover rice, I would first melt cheese and butter; then I would add chopped onions and peppers. When it was ready, I would pour the mixture over the rice and bake it. **TA-DA!** Cheesy rice!

For family entertainment (and to give my daughters some sense of normalcy), I would pack a bag of sandwiches and fruits and head to the local park. We would play and run around for hours before going back home. On the weekends, we would sometimes visit the museums. My oldest would bring her notebook and take notes on what she learned. Those things became part of our family's traditions.

CHAPTER SIXTY-TWO

It was my oldest daughter's birthday weekend in April 2005. The weather was beautiful and the sun was shining brightly. My daughter was excited because she had received the bicycle she asked for. Around noon, she asked if she could go outside to ride her new bike. I still wasn't comfortable with them opening the door and going outside – even for a few minutes – but since it was her birthday, I figured, *"Why not relax a little and let her enjoy her day?"*

I was sitting on the edge of the bed when she came back into the room and said, *"Mama, there is a poster on our door."* I said, **"Poster?" Immediately** my heart dropped. I couldn't breathe. I didn't want her to see the fear on my face. I was too scared to move and too scared to sit still. I went to the front door and sure enough, attached to the door was a white poster that read:

"Happy Birthday, girls – from Daddy. I love you and I miss you. Love, Jamal."

I snatched the poster off the door and made my daughter come back into the house. I locked the doors, closed the curtains, went into the bedroom, and dialed 911. When the police arrived, they said they would issue a warrant for his arrest because he had violated the Restraining Order. (I would later find out there is a **BIG** difference between Civil and Criminal Restraining Orders. Jamal's was Civil – which meant the law wasn't going to be overly-aggressive in pursuing charges against him.)

I packed the kids up and prepared to shut the house down tight. I called my friend in a panic and she said we could come stay with her for a couple of days.

The cycle of me not sleeping started all over again – even while at her house. I sat in her kitchenette and watched the glistening water on the lake all night long. I became an expert at moving around her house without making any noise. I would sleep for two hours at the **most** and then start my day. After the fourth day, I decided it was time to go back home.

There was something in me that whispered: ***STOP RUNNING. If he wanted to kill you, he would have when he put that poster on the door.***

I packed the girls up – shaky hands and all – and returned home.

CHAPTER SIXTY-THREE

After the first trip to court, I realized I needed to get myself **and** my information together. I began to focus on what I could do – and that was research. I was always good at that, so I decided to put my skills to work. Call me "Jo-Jo the Private Eye"!

In the beginning, I felt bad about finding information on Jamal, but the more I found out, the more obsessed I became with getting to the bottom of the truth. My reality became that I had no inkling of who the man was that I married. The only thing I knew for sure was that his name was Jamal.

I started my research by recalling all of the things he had told me about his past. *Was there anything there that could help me get a divorce?* I still had access to our emails, and it was there that I found out he had written the Bishop and Elder to have me removed from the denomination. He told them I was crazy, mentally-ill, and that I purposely set out to destroy his ministry.

He also told them I had kidnapped the children and that the reason he was not at church the last couple of Sundays was because he was busy working with the FBI and the police because I had taken the kids across the state line. (*I would later find out he had reported all of that to the police. I had to place a call to prove that I did **not** kidnap them and explain the **exact** reasons why I left.*)

During my 'Private Eye' stage, I found that he was on several dating websites – both while we were together **and** immediately after I left him. This revelation fueled me to press harder and deeper to find out even more about his deceitful life. His profile was almost always the same: Single father of a preemie seeking supportive woman – preferably non-Black; Pastor with a history of a broken heart looking for the right woman to share her life with him and his daughter; and wife left him for another man. There was one common theme on **all** of his profiles: His date of birth was different on each one.

I also found the emails he exchanged with the women.

One was even named "JoJo". She was of a different race, and he was quickly falling in love with her. Their conversations included chatter about how it was refreshing to share such great times with someone who truly cared. His story was often the same: He married a young girl who tricked him into marriage. He gave her his all, and she destroyed him, broke him into pieces, and destroyed his ministries. He was asking the Good Lord for guidance, forgiveness, and understanding to get over her. He was looking for someone to be gentle with him and his daughter as he attempted to raise a preemie because his wife had abandoned him and his child for a drug dealer – and he had no idea where she was.

In the beginning, I wasn't sure how I felt about the information I was finding out. I was angry. I was confused. I had way too many emotions going on, and I had no idea how to direct them, where to put them, or how to address them. *He said he loved me, right? So why was he doing all of this? Why was he writing these women?* Some of the dating sites he signed up for the same week I left him. *Why was I upset? I wasn't with him. What should I care?* But I did care – and I couldn't understand why. The emotions were too much for me to handle. *Why was I feeling this way?* **WHY?** On top of everything else, I was going to have to figure out my emotions…while being scared for my life.

CHAPTER SIXTY-FOUR

Getting divorced was a **HELL** of a lot harder than getting married. I had to prove who I was in order to change my name on my license! It was then I learned even *more* about Jamal. In order to prove I was divorced, I needed more documentation.

I recalled a conversation we had – early on when we were dating – when he said that everyone he married had tricked him, left him, and always hurt him. He wanted to make sure I would not do that to him and he needed to know that he could trust me. Of course I wanted him to trust me. I wanted to be the one that never hurt him and was always there for him to help build his ministry. I wanted to be the best wife **ever**. I wanted to be different from all those other women.

I began to think about his other wives and realized I wanted to know more about them. I recalled the cities he lived in. I called the courts and requested marriage and birth certificates. I learned he really loved to get married. My call to Alabama was the most shocking. I realized Jamal was married to the wife in Alabama while he was married to me for about nine months! I also found out I wasn't wife number three; I was wife number **FIVE!**

I was stunned. I was speechless. I was at work the majority of the time when I found out his dirty little secrets – but who could I share my newfound information with at work when I'm supposed to be working?

I oftentimes worked in a daze. I would often make up my work at the last minute because I had spent my entire day researching and making phone calls, copies, and getting my evidence together that I needed for my divorce. *(It's a good thing I type fast.)*

Once I found out Jamal was still married to another woman and me at the same time, I set out finding all the information I could on how to obtain an annulment. Unfortunately, it is something only an attorney could do. I had my fair share of dealings with attorneys by this point, so I contacted the Legal Aid Department of North Carolina and presented them with my case.

I told my attorney (who, in the beginning, wanted nothing to do with me until I convinced her I both read and understood the law) I had done all the work. All she had to do was show up! Once she looked over my documents, she said, *"You are crazy! You did all of this work?" "Yes"*, I replied. *"You should be an attorney"*, she complimented.

The day of court arrived. I wasn't allowed inside the courtroom. When my attorney exited, she said my marriage was officially annulled and I was free to take my last name back. I hugged her so tight! She said, *"Literally... All I did was hand the judge your work. He was impressed that someone with no law experience did it!"*

I didn't care about that. All I cared about was **I COULD HAVE MY LAST NAME AGAIN!** Another step to freedom!

CHAPTER SIXTY-FIVE

A couple of months later after finding the 'Happy Birthday' poster on my front door, I received a phone call from the Department of Social Services. Apparently, a child abuse and sexual assault claim had been made against me. I was stunned and had no idea what to say. The worker said she couldn't tell me who reported it or why, but that she needed to meet me to get more information. We made arrangements to meet at the local McDonald's one day after I got off work because for some reason, she did **not** want to meet me at my house. My internal alarm started ringing **loudly**.

On the day of the meeting, I had picked the girls up from daycare. It was another day that I had tried to run out of the building before the front desk clerk could tell me I still owed them and that the kids couldn't return without payment received. I didn't want to hear that the baby was out of diapers and I would have to lie and say she would have some "tomorrow". I didn't have **any** money, my account was in the negative, and what the daycare didn't know was that I used cloth diapers at home so that I could save the disposable diapers for daycare. No money meant no diapers.

By the time we arrived at McDonald's, the baby was very upset and crying because her diaper was **soaking** wet. I couldn't change her because I didn't have a dry diaper to put on her. I was embarrassed as I sat there being asked personal questions about my life while my child was wet up to her neck in the only diaper she had.

The worker began telling me about the accusations levied against me: I was a horrible parent. I only dated drug dealers. I subjected my oldest to drunkards and drugs…and the person who called was *sure* she had been touched inappropriately.

I just sat there. I didn't know what to say. It was surreal. I started to cry and told her everything from the beginning. She sat there in silence listening to my every word. When she spoke, she said, *"I didn't believe a word of what was told to me anyway. The person who came in scared me half to death – telling these stories about you. I felt uneasy being in a room with that person. I'm not supposed to tell you who reported you, but I'm going to: It was your husband."* The worker also shared with me that he had changed cars, advised me to please be careful, and to take all necessary precautions because she was afraid for me and my children's lives.

While at McDonald's, she interviewed my oldest daughter and we made arrangements for a home visit. I had to take a day off from work to meet the Social Worker. She told me the entire process would take a month and that she would make it as painless as possible. She also said my daughter would need to be checked by a medical doctor to ensure nothing inappropriate had been done to her.

The Social Worker recommended that I leave my home for a while and move the girls somewhere safe because she wasn't sure we were safe in my home. She thought we were in danger and she wanted to do her best to make sure nothing happened to us. I called my mother and she took the girls in while I stayed with a friend. After about a week, it was too much to expect my parents to take care of my girls, so I went back to get them and we went home.

I was **tired** of running. I was **tired** of leaving my house. I was completely tired of living like *that*.

CHAPTER SIXTY-SIX

The night before the Social Worker's scheduled home visit, I had done a deep cleaning with what little there was to clean. My purple couch, the wooden mattress my aunt had given me from when she was young, and my floor model TV received the royal cleaning treatment. (That was the complete list of furniture I had in the house.)

The worker called to say she was on her way and would arrive shortly. I put on the best clothes I had, looked at myself in the mirror, and prepared for her visit.

A knock came to the door. I never opened a door, looked out the front door, or even the front window without first going into the 3rd bedroom and peeking out the window. I saw a green car in the driveway – the **exact color car** the worker told me Jamal had changed in to. I started having trouble breathing. I looked out onto the porch and all I saw was a light-skinned heavy-set person with a close haircut. I went into complete hysteria!

I dialed 911 and said, *"My husband is outside my door and is here to kill me! Please send someone right away!"*

The knocking on the door got louder…and harder…and louder…and harder. The 911 operator said an officer was on the way and promptly disconnected the call. I could not believe he hung up on me! I called **right** back and screamed, *"Don't you understand? He will kill me! You cannot hang up on me until an officer arrives!"* The operator then placed me on hold. I was hiding in the bedroom closet with a death grip on the phone. When the operator returned to the line, my address was verified again and I was told the person at the front door is a Social Worker who was there for her appointment with me. I asked, *"How do you know that?"* He responded, *"She was on another call with a different operator screaming that you were inside the house dead and she knew who killed you."*

When I finally opened the door, both of us cried and hugged each other. Eventually, we started to laugh. The visit was as normal as could be. I was instructed to do two things:
1. Put at least two weeks' worth of food in the house; and
2. Have my daughter examined.

I didn't have the heart or nerve to say, *"I barely have food from day-to-day – let alone two weeks!"* Still, I knew I had to make that happen. Everything went according to plan, the doctor determined my daughter had **not** been touched inappropriately, and one month later, I was officially released from the supervision of Social Services.

CHAPTER SIXTY-SEVEN

Almost every morning when I left for work, the lady who lived at the end of the street would be outside in her yard raking the leaves or simply hanging outside. I never stopped or even waved at her. I had learned the hard way that not everyone is nice. I found it best to just mind my business.

My routine was simple: Go to work and come home. Once home, I didn't go out for *anything*.

One day, the lady from the end of the street stopped me on my way to work. She said, *"I don't know you, but the Lord told me to give you some clothes. Stop by here on your way home tonight."* I didn't know what else to say besides, *"Yes, ma'am."*

Her offer caused me to wonder: *Did she see me washing clothes out in the tub every night in order to have something clean to wear the next day?* That thought prompted another: *Did the people at my job realize I only had two pairs of pants and five shirts?*

When I made it home that night, my daughters and I walked across the street to the woman's house. When we entered her home, the living room was **full** of clothes that were just my size: coats, pants, sweaters, shirts, scarves, and shoes. It took me about six trips back and forth to get them all!

I wanted to cry, but I didn't want her asking me any questions. I told her, *"Thank you. I truly appreciate this. If there is anything I could do for you, please let me know."* (Since that day, we now have a friendship that is so strong. I cannot even begin to express the words of appreciation, adoration, and love I have for her. If I ever needed to know what a true Christian is, she is **IT**!)

Soon enough, I became comfortable enough with her to share my story. I told her and a few of my other neighbors so they would know if I gave the designated signal, they should call 911 for me because I was in trouble. Daily, my neighbor would call me at work to let me know the house was fine and that no one drove or stopped by in my absence. Then she would ask, *"So, what are you going to cook?"* My response was always, *"Whatever you would like for me to cook!"*

Over the years, this woman of God has adopted me and my daughters as her children. I know she prays for us daily. For over eight years now, I have cooked and shopped for her. We have hung out and she has become my best friend – and my oldest daughter's confidant and closest friend.

CHAPTER SIXTY-EIGHT

I swore I would *never* step foot back inside a church again, but I began to miss it; the hymns, the people…but I was still mad at God, so I wasn't going.

It took me a year to return to church. When I did, I sat on the last pew with a big hat – and before the sermon was over, I made sure the girls and I got up and left. That went on for about six months…until one day, the very observant pastor said (right at the end of his sermon), *"Sis. Jamal? Is that you?"*

I was rock-still. The church had over 1,000 members and on this Sunday, it was packed. *How in the **world** did he see me?* I was on the last pew **AND** I'm short. Everyone was taller than me, so I thought I was well-hidden. I didn't respond to his inquiry. He went on… "I see you leave every Sunday before I finish my sermon. Do you mind staying this time so that I can see you after service?" Of course I didn't have a choice after being called out like **that**!

I had no idea who that man was or how he knew who I was. I became really enraged with God because I wanted to know why He let me come to church only to be called out by one of Jamal's friends? By the time the pastor gave the Benediction, I had already determined he was going to call Jamal and tell him I was there. I was in the early stages of a full panic attack. The baby was crying and my oldest kept asking me how the man knew us.

After service, the pastor introduced himself, asked how I was doing, and inquired about Jamal. I told him the bare minimum: Jamal and I were separated. (*I would later email him and tell him the entire story – only for him to say he wasn't sure he could believe all of those things happened.*)

Well, thank you pastor, for not believing.

I stopped going to church again. I did not have the energy to expend trying to convince **ANYONE** I was telling the truth – that Jamal really did those horrible and ungodly things to me.

Eventually, I started going back to church – but I continued to sit in the back and left before service was over. I also always parked one street over from the church and backed the car in to its space so no one could see my tag or take special notice of my car.

CHAPTER SIXTY-NINE

One of the perks of participating in the Back-to-Work Program was it opened the door to another program that helped individuals purchase vehicles with a downpayment of only $500.00. I had to attend a one-day class, tell them my needs, pay my deposit, and they, in turn, provided me with a 1997 blue Honda Accord station wagon – in **excellent** condition.

The Honda was a blessing because the red Dodge Neon was beyond unsafe…with a wheel falling off, it not being able to hold more than $10.00 worth of gas (after I got it fixed), the dashboard was inoperable (so I never knew how fast I was driving), and no air conditioning.

I held onto that Neon as long as I possibly could…

CHAPTER SEVENTY

One morning, I woke up and simply decided I wanted more… I just wasn't sure what that "more" was.

I remember watching a University of Phoenix (UOP) video. I called the university on one of my sleepless nights. What else did I have to do anyway?

I had two friends in particular who I called religiously and they would listen to me talk all night (*bless their hearts*). Both knew when to listen to my painful rants and when I needed a distraction from what was on my mind with their interaction with me. That night was not comprised of **either** situation.

Anyway, back to UOP. After that initial phone call in the middle of the night, I was officially an MBA student!

I had no idea what I was doing or how I was going to do it. What I did know was that I wanted **something** more.

On the days I had school, my day started at 5:00 a.m. as usual with my commute. On the way back home, I would have to take the girls 30 minutes **past** my school to the babysitter and make it to school in time for class. Class let out at 10:00. By the time I drove to pick up the girls, it was after 11:00 when we made it home.

One of the ladies I worked with had a daughter who volunteered to babysit for me. The girl was only 14 at the time. Her mother would meet me at the local Boys and Girls Club to pick up my kids. The baby was so picky. If I wasn't near her, she would scream and cry until she threw up. Every week, I was dealing with that. I had to drive away listening to my child scream as I went off to school.

Oftentimes, I didn't have a sitter and had to find one at the last minute – which meant driving even further out of the way and racing back to the other side of town to be on time for class.

I tried to portray a normal life in front of my classmates. While they were laughing during breaks and talking about trips and other fun things, I was wondering if eating a piece of bread for dinner would hold me until the next day or where I was going to find money for diapers before school the next morning.

Other times, I was giving myself **HELL**. *Who was I to go back to school? I didn't have the money nor the time to go to school. Why did I need an MBA anyway?* The answer was always: *Because Jamal called me stupid and I had to prove to him that I was not stupid. I had to graduate with Honors. I had to.* **Nothing else would do.**

CHAPTER SEVENTY-ONE

Graduation day from UOP was amazing! My family and friends came to help me celebrate. I cried during the entirety of the graduation service. I mean I **CRIED**! People around me kept telling me to be quiet.

The celebrity guest speaker, Rhonda Watts, was talking about believing in yourself, following your dreams, and never letting anyone tell you that you cannot achieve. It was as if she was speaking directly to me!

When my name was called, the person directing us said to me, *"Speed up; we are behind!"* I looked at her and said, **"NO! I worked too hard to walk fast across this stage."**

That was the best walk **EVER** – hearing my name called followed by "…with a Master in Business with a Concentration in Healthcare".

I felt like I was **finally** finding the 'more' I was seeking!

Life was beginning to take on a new outlook. The sun was warm, the air was fresh, the looking over my shoulder was *almost* gone, the nightmares were down to once every three months, the self-confidence was being renewed. Just **life**…I wasn't as afraid as I used to be. I was just "being" – and that feeling was AMAZING!

CHAPTER SEVENTY-TWO

After Jamal violated his Restraining Order twice (once by showing up at my house and another by mailing me a letter), I had to go back to court after a year to get an extension. It was then that all my hard work had paid off.

My family was able to come with me on that day to support me. Don't get me wrong: I was still scared. I was still very nervous, but I wasn't as afraid as I was the first time I had to go to court. I walked into the courtroom with a hot pink suit, heels, and a briefcase full of questions and evidence.

When Jamal walked in, there was nowhere for him to sit – except beside my parents. He chose to stand. When he entered, he was not the man I remembered. He had on jeans (which he **never** wore) and a t-shirt. The Jamal I knew was always immaculate with both his looks and clothing.

We both walked to our tables in front of the judge and waited for him to tell us how to proceed. The judge allowed me to go first. He asked me why I was there and what did I have to say to the court about extending my Restraining Order.

I told the judge I had a packet of information for him that would explain why I needed the extension and how Jamal had violated the Order. He asked if I wanted to enter it as evidence and I responded, **"*Of course!*"** I gave a copy to the judge and he said, *"Well, let's have Mr. Jamal read it first so he can read the allegations against him."* I told the judge that wouldn't be necessary because I brought a copy for Jamal to have for himself. I walked over to Jamal's table and handed him his copy of the documents.

After everyone read it, the judge stated it was clear to him that I had done my work and he was pleasantly surprised. He asked me a few questions before he moved on to Jamal. When it was Jamal's turn, he asked to be dismissed to take his medicine with water. The judge said, *"There is water on the table."* Jamal replied, *"I don't want that water. I want to take my medicine outside the courtroom."* The judge said that was unnecessary and insane, but he granted him a few minutes to go take his medicine outside the courtroom and then return.

When he returned, he tried to convince the judge that I was crazy, that I lied to him, and that I tricked him. At every turn, the judge stopped him and said, *"I would like for you to ask questions like Ms. Jamal did and then answer them like she did. I don't want to hear your stories."*

I wanted to laugh, but I held a straight face…until the judge granted me my Restraining Order for another year. I showed ALL of my pearly whites! Court was then dismissed.

I have to say this: Walking out of that courtroom on that day in my **HOT** pink suit was one of the best feelings **EVER**!

CHAPTER SEVENTY-THREE

Raising my daughters on my own, I became determined for them to experience new things, to see things in a different way – and to feel safe at **any** cost. I wanted them to be ladies – women with character and a solid foundation. I never wanted a man to tell them they were not good enough or smart enough.

Every day was a learning day. Every day we read scriptures on the way to daycare and discussed what the passages meant. Every day we talked about what it meant to be a lady – to be a woman amongst women. We talked about how to talk – how to articulate words. We talked about how to walk, dress appropriately, be respectful, and be respected – at **ALL** times.

I was adamant about them keeping their word and how, at all times, their word was the only thing people would accept. I made sure to drill in the fact that actions always have a reaction – and some have severe consequences.

Sometimes I wanted to cry. I didn't want to be so hard on them, but I refused to let them live the life I did. I **refused** – and that meant I learned some lessons right along with them.

CHAPTER SEVENTY-FOUR

About two years after leaving Jamal, I had settled into a steady routine: children, work, school. I was actually feeling a little bit better about life!

But then...

It was a usual night. The kids were asleep by 9:00 p.m. and I relaxed until 10:00 p.m. At 10:00, I settled down on the couch with my laptop to do my homework. Suddenly, there was a knock on the door.

I didn't have a weapon (*and I was too scared to scream or run*), so I peeked out the office window and saw a police car. I called 911 and verified the officer's presence before opening the door and letting him in. I was thinking all kinds of things that could be wrong – *like who was dead?* – until he opened his mouth and told me he was there looking for **ME**!

I was totally confused. I asked, *"Why are you looking for me?"* He then asked me, *"Do you remember an attorney you hired and paid with a check?"* I went to retrieve my checkbook, came back, and told him, *"No, I didn't write a check to an attorney."* We were sitting on the couch talking when it hit me: He was talking about the attorney I found who was going to help me with the Restraining Order against Jamal. I had written him a check for $500.00 as a Retainer Fee. I clearly recall asking him to cash it **immediately**, but it was over a month later before he did. Needless to say, the money wasn't there when he attempted to cash the check.

He asked for repayment at a time when I didn't have the money. As time went on, I simply forgot about it. He never sent another request, and I completely forgot about him and the money he was owed – until 10:00 p.m. that night with the police officer on my couch.

The officer was so kind. He said to me, *"I am going to have to take you in. They have a warrant for your arrest."* I asked, *"What about my kids?"* He responded, *"We can call Social Services."*

I started to panic. I was **NOT** going to do that, so I called my neighbor and gave her a quick update of my situation. She told me to bring the children right over, so I woke them up and took them across to the street.

The officer **assured** me that the *only* things I needed to bring were my debit and ID cards. I could pay my bond and be on my way back home in no time. That gave me some relief. By 10:30 p.m., I was in the back of the police car and on my way to jail. When we arrived, the officer made sure to handcuff me before we went in. The Booking Agent at the jail had the nerve to ask me out on a date *"...if I was going to be free tomorrow night"*. I told him, *"Sir, I am going to jail. How can you possibly ask me out on a date?"* The woman who took my mug shot gave me directions – ones I thought I had followed to the letter – until the officers started to laugh at me and told me I was standing the wrong way. They hated that I was there, but it was part of their job...

I was placed in a holding cell – directly across from a man who thought he was Jesus Christ. He kept saying how he could kill himself and then come back to life. I just sat there staring at the wall while listening to him rant about being a Black man and the problems he faced.

Eventually, one of the guards came to get me to tell me I was allowed my one phone call. They also informed me that I would be going before the Magistrate Judge that evening. The judge told me a couple of things I wished the officer would have correctly relayed to me: First, they **don't** take debit cards – it's CASH ONLY; and secondly, you cannot use **anything** inside the building (ATMs included) to pay your bail.

So, I had money to bail out of jail, but I couldn't use the ATM machine to access it. That meant I had to spend the night in jail until someone could come to retrieve my debit card, get the money from my account, and post my bail.

I remember how humiliating it was to go into a room with an officer, be stripped down, and allow them to inspect me to ensure I wasn't hiding drugs or weapons in "unknown" places.

After that 'violation', I was given an orange jumpsuit, slide-on shoes, and a bag that contained underwear, toothpaste, toothbrush, two sheets, and a folded mat. I was ushered into the holding cell and, because it was so late, I had the privilege of placing my mat at the top of the stairs on the floor and that is where I slept.

The next morning, I brushed my teeth and breakfast was served. It was something just like we see on TV: a big woman sat beside me and asked me if I wanted my breakfast (which was a boiled egg, a slice of white bread, and grits). I told her "no". She nicely took my plate as I just stared down at my hands.

I couldn't believe that on the day before, I had picked up my oldest from school early and surprised her by treating her to getting our nails painted together and made a visit to the ice cream shop. Yes: I splurged.

I looked at my hands and the pink polish while thinking, *"I must be dreaming. This cannot be real!"*

My first phone call was to my parents – and they were just as surprised as I was. They lived over 300 miles away, so help from them could not be immediate.

I found out really quick that your time is not your own. Every two hours, the jail went on lockdown. That meant we all had to go into our cells and lay down or do *whatever* for 45 minutes until we were able to have free time again. The jailer would often come to the door and call someone's name. I would rush them and ask about me. All they would tell me was, ***"Not yet. Have a seat."***

Eventually, my parents couldn't accept my calls anymore because collect calls were costly. I was able to get in touch with some friends who came to get my debit card, go the bank to get the bail money, and post my bail. First, however, I had to go before the judge. When my name was called, I was handcuffed by the wrists and ankles and taken into another room to stand before a TV screen to speak to the judge. I really never opened my mouth. It all went so fast. All I know was that she said bail was posted, fines were paid, and I was free to go. **HOWEVER**, my freedom came with a great price: a felony on my record. Although I can explain **why** I have a felony, I still wish it wasn't there.

Again, another lesson learned. It left me thinking that Jesus **must** really have a lot of faith in me because the problems just kept coming and coming.

My friends later told me that even though they emptied both my checking and savings accounts, it wasn't enough money. They all pitched in and made up the difference. I cried because that was all the money I had – and it had taken forever to save that. I knew I was going to have to do something extra to make sure I paid them back.

Thankfully, my daughters were taken to and picked up from school – and had no idea what my night entailed.

Needless to say: Lesson learned for me…no checks – **EVER!**

CHAPTER SEVENTY-FIVE

Jamal did reach out to me. He mailed a letter to the only address he had for me: the former church member's home. When I saw the letter with his name on it, my hands instantly started to sweat. I was too scared to open it. I was mad at myself for letting that feeling overwhelm me, for allowing it to take my breath away, and for having that feeling in the pit of my stomach. I was having those, *"So, this is how I am going to die?"* thoughts.

The letter was pages and pages of him telling me that I should forgive him and give him his family back. He said he loved me and the girls and that he promised never to hit me again...if I would just come back.

It didn't end there, though... At the end of the letter, he listed the rules that we would have to abide by in order to be together again.

He stated there was no need to remember the past. He prayed that God forgave me for treating **him** badly. He actually had the **audacity** to write, *"Was I really that bad? Didn't I deserve love and to have my family back again?"* I chose to not respond to him at all.

CHAPTER SEVENTY-SIX

I found a book called *The Battlefield of the Mind* by Joyce Meyer at a consignment shop and started to read it. It was about dealing with depression, self-doubt, having self-confidence, and learning self-talk – and how to overcome all of that with the Word of God. I began to study every single page. I **needed** something to make sense to me. I **needed** someone to give me an answer to something, and for a moment, her book did just that.

Today, that book *still* sits on my nightstand. I write in my journal daily. When I have a low day or begin to question what I am doing or why I am sharing my story, I go back and read where I came from. I read my favorite scriptures, speak out loud, and remind myself of who I am. I have an affirmation that hangs on my mirror in my bedroom that I read daily as well.

It took me some time to realize my story – in all of its realness and raw beauty – wasn't about bragging; it was about being confident and acknowledging that I wasn't who Jamal said I was.

CHAPTER SEVENTY-SEVEN

Take it from a survivor: Speaking positive things to yourself and about yourself is a *wonderful* thing. It enables you to focus on who you really are. You begin to realize that life is an amazing thing! You now have a fresh start to live your life the way you want to live it.

The hardest part will be letting go – letting go of the anger, hurt, frustration, and unfairness. It is a process…a difficult one at that. It was a daily task that required **action – NOT JUST PRAYER.** The journey is not pretty; it is hard!

When you become a survivor, you need a different level of support than you do when you first leave your abuser. The support I need now is to be surrounded by other survivors and be encouraged that the path I have now chosen is not only for me, but for that woman who is now **ME**.

The woman standing at the door.

The woman locked in a room for eight hours.

The woman who was told she was a horrible mother, wife, and person.

The woman who looks in the mirror and sees a damaged woman and scars beyond repair.

I am her.

She is me.

I will continue to be her until she can be who she is meant to be in totality.

CHAPTER SEVENTY-EIGHT

There were some things I had to come to realize about myself and about life. I had to learn that you have to rest in what God has given you. You have to learn that it is okay to be different. You **are** different. The most important thing to remember about abusers and manipulators is that they see something in you that you don't see. They **want** to be a part of you because you are beyond amazing. However, in order to be a part of you, they need to be in the position to control that part of you so that you don't share or develop it…and then leave them. They are both jealous and selfish individuals.

The hardest part of my journey up to this point has been for me to **NOT** retaliate against Jamal, not write responses to his articles (yes, he's been writing terrible lies about me publicly to this very day), and to not say anything…just let it go. On those days when the desire is overwhelming to say something, I want to pay him back horribly – but I don't.

Instead, in those moments of turmoil and weakness, I ask God to climb into His lap or to hide behind Him for a just a few minutes until I get myself together.

How I see God is totally different. My relationship with God is now different. It has grown from a mustard seed into a strong, weight-bearing tree. I can't see the top of the tree, but I know it's there. I only get to see the base of the tree, but it's so peaceful and relaxing under the shade of the tree. I ease into the moment and let go of whatever is holding me back so that when I have to leave the shade and security of the tree, I am no longer carrying the burdens I came with.

CHAPTER SEVENTY-NINE

I now have the opportunity to share my story with other women. I never know how I am going to start or what I am going to say, but the words always seem to be the ones needed to be said.

I always finish with a group by giving them a pen and paper. I ask them to do one thing: When they wake up in the morning, write down one thing they are going to do differently today than they did the day before. It doesn't matter how big or small – just write it down. After 30 days, they will find they have a book of changes and new beginnings. They will also find that during the month, they have actually written a book of positive things that have been accomplished. As such, they have begun to replace the negative things they used to say and believe about themselves.

I encourage you to do the same. Whenever you feel discouraged, take out the book and look at the small changes made that make your life different.

I know the questions on everyone's minds are: **What happened to Jamal? Where is he now? Has he talked to or communicated with you since?**

Well, it would be nice if the story ended right there…

Of course it doesn't!

Being **FEARLESS** does **not** mean we are not afraid, scared, or unsure. It means that we feel those things and understand them. We are going to breathe it in, feel it, look at it in the face, and put it in a place.

Second by second of every day, make an effort to break it down to its finest compound – then build a new memory to replace "it".

Let's be **FEARLESS**…together.

COMING SOON

BE FEARLESS MOVEMENT

It is my **PURPOSE** to help others understand that being **FEARLESS** is possible.

Keep an eye out for the ***BE FEARLESS*** T-shirt line, journals, daily inspiration, and a support group for survivors!

ABOUT THE AUTHOR

J'Anmetra "Jo-Jo" Waddell is a strong advocate for victims and survivors of domestic violence. As a formerly abused Preacher's Wife, she speaks candidly about the issues of domestic violence and abuse with emphasis on empowering individuals who are victims and survivors of abuse. By educating and bringing awareness to the community, she believes survivors are the teachers who can carry the message of education, awareness, and empowerment to their families and communities.

In 2016, J'Anmetra's book, *Fearless Woman: Born to Give Thanks*, was awarded Author of the Year – Drama Category by the Writer's Ball. She has been a featured speaker on Blog Talk Radio – *"Let's Chat with Mz Toni and Lissha – Fantaasy…Fiction…or Life"*, on *"This Needs to Be Said TV"* with Katherine Waddell, and *Ashes to Beauty: Blooming Into Your Purpose* with La Deema Burns. She has been a Guest Speaker at the Uninhibited Woman Spring Retreat in 2016; The Greatest Comeback Ever with Kim Cole in 2015; at Emory University / IAAP from 2012-2014; Spring to Life 2015; and Guest Panelist for Rose of Sharon's SHAME NO MORE even in 2015.

J'Anmetra is the Owner/CEO of *Bare Your Hair* – a haircare line for those who suffer from Alopecia, thinning hair, and bald spots.

BARE YOUR HAIR was a featured vendor at the Steve Harvey Neighborhood Awards in 2014.

Shop for ALL products at:
www.BareYourHair.com

CONTACT INFORMATION:
J'Anmetra L. Waddell, MBA/HCM
www.BeAFearless.com
Email: **janmetra@beafearless.com**
Speaking/Business Inquiries: **janmetra@gmail.com**

APPENDIX

The following is supporting documentation of Author J'Anmetra "Jo-Jo" Waddell's dealings with the court system as it related to her Domestic Violence case against Pastor "Jamal".

(To protect the privacy of the Defendant, his true name and other personal identifying information have been removed.)

STATE OF NORTH CAROLINA

~~~~~~~~~~ County

Name Of Plaintiff
Shirla L

VERSUS

Name And Address Of Defendant

Fayetteville NC 28304

File No.

In The General Court Of Justice
District Court Division

**NOTICE OF HEARING
ON DOMESTIC VIOLENCE
PROTECTIVE ORDER**

G.S. 50B-2

To The Defendant Named Above:

The attached Complaint has been filed alleging that you have committed acts of domestic violence against the plaintiff and/or the plaintiff's minor child(ren).

☐ 1. The attached Ex Parte Order has been issued against you. If you violate the Order, you are subject to being held in contempt or being charged with the crime of violating this Ex Parte Order. A hearing will be held before a district court judge at the date, time and location indicated below. At that hearing it will be determined whether the Order will be continued.

☐ 2. A hearing will be held before a district court judge at the date, time and location indicated below. At that hearing it will be determined whether emergency relief in protecting the plaintiff and the plaintiff's child(ren) should be granted.

Date Of Hearing: 8-5-04   Time Of Hearing: 9:00 ☒ AM ☐ PM   Date: 7-29-04

Location Of Hearing: 9A

Signature

☐ Deputy CSC   ☒ Assistant CSC   ☐ Clerk Of Superior Court

NOTE TO CLERK: If the first block is checked, the hearing must be scheduled within ten (10) days of the issuance of the Ex Parte Order or seven (7) days from date of service on defendant, whichever occurs later. If the second block is checked, the defendant must be given five (5) days notice of the hearing. Give or mail a copy of the Notice to the plaintiff.

RETURN OF SERVICE

I certify that this Notice and a copy of the Complaint ☐ and the Ex Parte Order were received and served on the defendant as follows:

Date Served   Name Of Defendant

☐ 1. By delivering to the defendant named above a copy of this Notice of Hearing and a copy of the Complaint ☐ and the Ex Parte Order in this action.

☐ 2. By leaving a copy of this Notice of Hearing and a copy of the Complaint ☐ and the Ex Parte Order in this action at the defendant's dwelling house or usual place of abode with a person of suitable age and discretion then residing therein.

Name And Address Of Person With Whom Copies Left

☐ Defendant WAS NOT served for the following reason:

Date Received   Date Of Return   Name Of Sheriff

County Of Sheriff   Deputy Sheriff Making Return

AOC-CV-306, Rev. 6/2000
© 2000 Administrative Office of the Courts

STATE OF NORTH CAROLINA

Wake
~~Cumberland~~ County

Name Of Plaintiff: _Rhonda L._

Address:
City, State, Zip: _Raleigh NC 29604_

Name Of Defendant: _____
VERSUS

Fayetteville NC 28401

File No. _____

In The General Court Of Justice
District Court Division

CIVIL SUMMONS
DOMESTIC VIOLENCE

☐ ALIAS AND PLURIES SUMMONS

G.S. 1A-1, Rules 3, 4

Date Original Summons Issued: _____

Date(s) Subsequent Summons(es) Issued: _____

To The Defendant Named Below:
Name And Address Of Defendant

A Civil Action Has Been Commenced Against You!

You are notified to appear and answer the complaint of the plaintiff as follows:

1. Serve a copy of your written answer to the complaint upon the plaintiff or plaintiff's attorney within thirty (30) days after you have been served. You may serve your answer by delivering a copy to the plaintiff or by mailing it to the plaintiff's last known address; and

2. File the original of the written answer with the Clerk of Superior Court of the county named above.

If you fail to answer the complaint, the plaintiff will apply to the Court for the relief demanded in the complaint.

Name And Address Of Plaintiff's Attorney (If None, Address Of Plaintiff)

Date Issued: _07/29/04_   Time: _1:52_ ☐ AM ☒ PM

Signature: _____
☐ Deputy CSC   ☐ Assistant CSC   ☐ Clerk Of Superior Court

☐ **ENDORSEMENT**
This Summons was originally issued on the date indicated above and returned not served. At the request of the plaintiff, the time within which this Summons must be served is extended sixty (60) days.

Date Of Endorsement: _____   Time: _____ ☐ AM ☐ PM

Signature: _____
☐ Deputy CSC   ☐ Assistant CSC   ☐ Clerk Of Superior Court

AOC-CV-217, Rev. 10/01
© 2001 Administrative Office of the Courts   (Over)

STATE OF NORTH CAROLINA

_____ County

Name Of Plaintiff (Person Filing Complaint)

Annitia

VERSUS

Name And Address Of Defendant (Person Accused Of Abuse)

_____

Fayetteville, NC 28301

File No. _____

In The General Court Of Justice
District Court Division

**COMPLAINT AND MOTION
FOR
DOMESTIC VIOLENCE
PROTECTIVE ORDER**

G.S. 50B-1, -2, -3, -4

(Check only boxes that apply and fill in blanks. Additional sheets may be attached.)

1. I live in _____ County, North Carolina.
2. The defendant and I ☐ are married. ☐ are divorced.
   ☐ are persons of the opposite sex who are not married but live together or have lived together.
   ☑ have a child in common.
   ☐ are parent and child or grandparent and grandchild.
   ☐ are current or former household members.
   ☐ are persons of the opposite sex who are in or have been in a dating relationship.
3. There ☐ is ☑ is not another court proceeding between the defendant and me pending in this or any other state.
   (List county, state and what kind of proceeding, if applicable.)

☐ 4. The defendant has attempted to cause or has intentionally caused me bodily injury; or has placed me or a member of my family or household in fear of imminent serious bodily injury or in fear of continued harassment that rises to such a level as to inflict substantial emotional distress; or has committed a sexual offense against me in that: (Give specific dates and describe in detail what happened.)

Last incident of assault was on _____. After the last time I left the house and returned he told me that if I ever tried to take his child away from him he would kill me. On Saturday the _____ he threatened to harm me or that he would take money to take care of the child and not _____ about me.

☐ 5. The defendant has attempted to cause or has intentionally caused bodily injury to the child(ren) living with me or in my custody; has placed my child(ren) in fear of imminent serious bodily injury or in fear of continued harassment that rises to such a level as to inflict substantial emotional distress; or has committed a sexual offense against the child(ren) in that: (Give specific dates and describe in detail what happened.)

N/A

☑ 6. I believe there is danger of serious and immediate injury to me or my children.
☑ 7. (Check this block if you ask for temporary child custody.) The defendant and I are the parents of the following children under the age of eighteen.
A COPY OF "AFFIDAVIT AS TO STATUS OF MINOR CHILD" (AOC-CV-609) MUST BE ATTACHED FOR EACH CHILD.

Name	Date Of Birth	Name	Date Of Birth

(Over)

AOC-CV-303, Rev. 12/03, Page 1 of 3
© 2003 Administrative Office of the Courts

	VERSUS		File No

Name Of Defendant

- [ ] 13. I want the Court to order the defendant to surrender to the sheriff his/her firearms, ammunition, and gun permits to purchase a firearm and carry a concealed weapon.
- [x] 14. I want the defendant to be ordered to attend an abuser treatment program.
- [ ] 15. I want the defendant to be ordered to provide me and the children suitable alternative housing.
- [ ] 16. I want the defendant to be ordered to make payments for my support as required by law, but I understand it is only *temporary* and that I must file a separate action for regular permanent spousal support.
- [ ] 17. Other: (specify)

Date: 7/29/04

Signature Of Plaintiff (Person Filing Complaint)

VERIFICATION

I, the undersigned, being first duly sworn, say that I am the plaintiff in this action; that I have read the Complaint and Motion; that the matters and things alleged in the Complaint and Motion are true except as to those things alleged upon information and belief and as to those I believe them to be true and accurate.

SWORN AND SUBSCRIBED TO BEFORE ME

Date: 7/29/04

Signature Of Plaintiff

Date | Signature

- [ ] Deputy CSC
- [ ] Assistant CSC
- [ ] Clerk of Superior Court
- [ ] Designated Magistrate

Name Of Plaintiff (Type Or Print)

SEAL [ ] Notary

Date My Commission Expires

AOC-CV-303, Rev. 12/03, Page 3 of 3
© 2003 Administrative Office of the Courts

STATE OF NORTH CAROLINA

_____Wake_____ County

In The General Court Of Justice
District Court Division

Court File No.

Name And Address Of Plaintiff
J'Ammetia L.
Raleigh NC 27606

VERSUS

Name And Address Of Defendant
Fayetteville, NC 28314

AFFIDAVIT AS TO STATUS OF MINOR CHILD

G.S. 50A-9

Name Of Minor Child			
Date Of Birth		Birthplace	

I, the undersigned affiant, being first duly sworn, say that during the past five (5) years the above named minor child has lived as follows:

Period Of Residence		Address	Name Of Person Lived With	Present Address Of Person
From	To			
7/26/14	Present	Bent Pine Drive Fyt 28314		Bent Pine Drive Fayt 28314
5/7	6/18	Vann St. Raleigh 27606		N/A

I further say that: (Check those that apply)

☐ I have participated in litigation concerning the custody of the above named child.

Capacity As Participant	Date Of Action	Name And Address Of Court

Details

☐ I have information of a custody proceeding concerning the above named child pending in a court in this or another state.

Name And Address Of Court	Details

☐ I know of a person as listed below, who has physical custody or claims to have custody or visitation rights with respect to the above named child.

Name And Address Of Person	
	☐ Physical Custody
	☐ Claimed Custody
	☐ Visitation Rights

SWORN AND SUBSCRIBED TO BEFORE ME

Date: 7/29/21

Signature Of Affiant

Name Of Affiant (Type Or Print): J'Ammetia L.

Relationship To Above Named Child: mother

Date: 7/29/21

Signature Of Person Authorized To Administer Oaths

☐ Deputy CSC   ☐ Assistant CSC   ☐ Clerk Of Superior Court

Date Commission Expires

SEAL   ☐ Notary

AOC-CV-609, Rev. 6/2000
© 2000 Administrative Office of the Courts

Case No. 04CV___	DOMESTIC VIOLENCE
Court: General Court of Justice District Court Division	ORDER OF PROTECTION
County: Wake State: NC	☐ CONSENT ORDER

G.S. 50B-2, -3, -3.1

PETITIONER/PLAINTIFF
First: T'Anmetra   Middle: ___   Last: ___

PETITIONER/PLAINTIFF IDENTIFIERS
Date Of Birth Of Petitioner: ___

And/or on behalf of minor family member(s). (list Name And DOB)

Other Protected Persons/DOB:

VERSUS

RESPONDENT/DEFENDANT
First: ___   Middle: ___   Last: ___

Relationship to Petitioner: ☑ spouse ☐ former spouse
☐ unmarried, of opposite sex, currently or formerly living together
☐ unmarried, have a child in common
☐ of opposite sex, currently or formerly in dating relationship
☐ current or former household member
☐ parent ☐ grandparent ☐ child ☐ grandchild

Respondent's/Defendant's Address:

RESPONDENT/DEFENDANT IDENTIFIERS

Sex	Race	DOB	HT	WT
M	Black	9/16/		240
Eyes	Hair	Social Security Number		
Blue				
Drivers License No.	State	Expiration Date		

Distinguishing Features:

CAUTION:
☐ Weapon Involved

THE COURT HEREBY FINDS THAT:
This matter was heard by the undersigned district court judge, the court has jurisdiction over the parties and subject matter, and the Respondent/Defendant has been provided with reasonable notice and opportunity to be heard.
Additional findings of this order are set forth on Page 2.

THE COURT HEREBY ORDERS THAT:
☑ The above named Respondent/Defendant shall not commit any further acts of abuse or make any threats of abuse.
☑ The above named Respondent/Defendant shall have no contact with the Petitioner/Plaintiff. No contact includes any defendant-initiated contact, direct or indirect, by means such as telephone, personal contact, email, pager, gift-giving or telefacsimile machine. [05]

Additional terms of this order are as set forth on Pages 3 and 4.

The terms of this order shall be effective until August 5, 2005

WARNINGS TO THE RESPONDENT/DEFENDANT:
This order shall be enforced, even without registration, by the courts of any state, the District of Columbia, and any U.S. Territory, and may be enforced by Tribal Lands (18 U.S.C. Section 2265). Crossing state, territorial, or tribal boundaries to violate this order may result in federal imprisonment (18 U.S.C. Section 2262).

Federal law makes it a crime for you to possess, transport, ship or receive any firearm or ammunition while this order is in effect even if this order does not prohibit you from possessing firearms. (18 U.S.C. Section 922(g)(8)).

This order will be enforced anywhere in North Carolina.

Only the Court can change this order. The plaintiff cannot give you permission to violate this order.

See additional warnings on Page 4.

AOC-CV-306, Page 1 of 4, Rev. 3/04
© 2004 Administrative Office of the Courts   (Over)

Transition to Freedom: Fearless Woman – Part Two

ADDITIONAL FINDINGS

1. Present at the hearing were: ☑ the plaintiff, represented by _pro se_ ☐ the defendant, represented by _served (no show)_

2. ☑ As indicated by the check block under Respondent/Defendant's name on Page 1, the parties are or have been in a personal relationship.

3. ☑ On (date of most recent conduct) _7/23/04_, the defendant
   - ☐ a. ☐ attempted to cause ☐ intentionally caused bodily injury to ☐ the plaintiff ☐ a minor child in the custody of the plaintiff
   - ☑ b. placed in fear of imminent serious bodily injury ☑ the plaintiff ☐ a member of the plaintiff's family ☐ a member of the plaintiff's household
   - ☐ c. placed in fear of continued harassment that rises to such a level as to inflict substantial emotional distress ☐ the plaintiff ☐ a member of plaintiff's family ☐ a member of plaintiff's household
   - ☑ d. committed an act defined in G.S. 14- ☐ 27.2 (1st deg. rape) ☐ 27.3 (2nd deg. rape) ☐ 27.4 (1st deg. sexual off.) ☐ 27.5 (2nd deg. sexual off.) ☑ 27.5A (sexual battery) ☐ 27.7 (sexual activity by substitute parent) against ☐ the plaintiff ☐ a child living with or in the custody of the plaintiff

   by (describe defendant's conduct) On July 23, 2004 the Deft told the Plaintiff he would "Kill her" if she tried to take the child and leave. Deft took Plaintiff's car keys, cell phone & bank card to prevent her from leaving.

4. ☐ The defendant is in possession of, owns or has access to firearms, ammunition, and gun permits described below. (Describe all firearms, ammunition, gun permits and give identifying number(s) if known, and indicate where defendant keeps firearms.)

   → On 7/24/04 the Deft forced the Plaintiff to have sex by holding her hostage and by intimidation and not allowing her to have her clothes and that he would paralyze her.

5. The defendant _does not own_ a gun to her knowledge.
   - ☐ a. ☐ used ☐ threatened to use a deadly weapon against the ☐ plaintiff ☐ minor child residing with or in the custody of the plaintiff
   - ☐ b. has a pattern of prior conduct involving the ☐ use ☐ threatened use of violence with a firearm against persons
   - ☐ c. made threats to seriously injure or kill the ☐ plaintiff ☐ minor child residing with or in the custody of the plaintiff
   - ☐ d. made threats to commit suicide
   - ☐ e. inflicted serious injuries upon the ☐ plaintiff ☐ minor child residing with or in the custody of the plaintiff in that (state facts)

6. ☑ The parties are the parents of the following children under the age of eighteen (18). The children are presently in the physical custody of the ☑ plaintiff ☐ defendant. The plaintiff has submitted an "Affidavit As To The Status Of The Minor Child." NOTE TO JUDGE: A copy of AOC-CV-609 for each child must be attached to the order.

Name	Sex	Date Of Birth	Name	Sex	Date Of Birth
—	F	4/1/—			

7. ☐ The ☐ defendant ☐ plaintiff is presently in possession of the parties' residence at _n/a_

8. ☐ The ☐ defendant ☑ plaintiff is presently in possession of the parties' vehicle described below: _1995 Dodge Neon_

9. ☑ Other: (specify) Due to the age of the minor child (3 months) the court finds it appropriate to grant Custody (w/o prejudice) to the Plaintiff during the period of this order and for the child's safety.

Name Of Defendant	File No. 04CV

CONCLUSIONS

Based on these facts, the Court makes the following conclusions of law:
- [x] 1. The defendant has committed acts of domestic violence against the plaintiff.
- [ ] 2. The defendant has committed acts of domestic violence against the minor child(ren) residing with or in the custody of the plaintiff.
- [x] 3. There is danger of serious and immediate injury to the [x] plaintiff [ ] minor child(ren). [G.S. 50B-2(b)]
- [x] 4. The Court has jurisdiction under the Uniform Child Custody Jurisdiction And Enforcement Act, and it is in the best interests of the minor child(ren) of the parties that temporary custody of them be given to the plaintiff.
- [x] 5. This domestic violence protective order is necessary to bring about a cessation of acts of domestic violence. [G.S. 50B-3(a)]
- [ ] 6. The defendant's conduct requires that he/she surrender all firearms, ammunition and gun permits. (G.S. 50B-3.1)
- [ ] 7. The plaintiff has failed to prove grounds for issuance of a domestic violence protective order.

ORDER

It is ORDERED that:
- [x] 1. the defendant shall not assault, threaten, abuse, follow, harass (by telephone, visiting the home or workplace or other means, *e-mail*), or interfere with the plaintiff. A law enforcement officer shall arrest the defendant if the officer has probable cause to believe the defendant has violated this provision. [01]
- [ ] 2. the defendant shall not assault, threaten, abuse, follow, harass (by telephone, visiting the home or workplace or other means), or interfere with the minor child(ren) residing with or in the custody of the plaintiff. A law enforcement officer shall arrest the defendant if the officer has probable cause to believe the defendant has violated this provision. [01]
- [x] 3. the defendant shall not threaten a member of the plaintiff's family or household. [02]
- [ ] 4. the plaintiff is granted possession of, and the defendant is excluded from, the parties' residence described above and all personal property located in the residence except for the defendant's personal clothing, toiletries and tools of trade. [03]
- [ ] 5. any law enforcement agency with jurisdiction shall evict the defendant from the residence and shall assist the plaintiff in returning to the residence. [08]
- [ ] 6. the [ ] plaintiff [08] [ ] defendant [08] is entitled to get personal clothing, toiletries, and tools of trade from the parties' residence. A law enforcement officer shall assist the [ ] plaintiff [ ] defendant in returning to the residence to get these items.
- [x] 7. the defendant shall stay away from the plaintiff's residence or any place where the plaintiff receives temporary shelter. A law enforcement officer shall arrest the defendant if the officer has probable cause to believe the defendant has violated this provision. [04]
- [x] 8. the defendant shall stay away from the following places:
  - [x] (a) the place where the plaintiff works. [04]
  - [x] (b) the child(ren)'s school. [04]
  - [x] (c) the place where the child(ren) receives day care. [04]
  - [x] (d) the plaintiff's school. [04]
  - [x] (e) Other: (name other places) [04] *Deft not to come w/in 200 yds of Plaintiff or minor child. Providing the Deft wants visitation w/ the minor child, the parties will need to exchange child through a third party.*
- [x] 9. the plaintiff is granted possession and use of the vehicle described on Page 2. [08]
- [x] 10. (Check this block only if Block No. 4 in Conclusions is checked.) the plaintiff is awarded temporary custody of the child(ren) named in Finding No. 6. [08]
- [x] 11. the defendant is ordered to make payments to the plaintiff for support of the minor child(ren) as required by law. [08]
- [ ] 12. The defendant is prohibited from [x] possessing, owning or receiving [07] [x] purchasing a firearm for the effective period of this Order [07] [ ] and the defendant's concealed handgun permit is suspended for the effective period of this Order. [08]
  - [ ] The defendant is a law enforcement officer/member of the armed services and [ ] may [ ] may not possess or use a firearm for official use.
- [ ] 13. the defendant surrender to the Sheriff serving this order the firearms, ammunition, gun permits described in block No. 4 of the Findings on Page 2 of this Order and any other firearms and ammunition in the defendant's care, custody, possession, ownership or control.

NOTE TO DEFENDANT: You must surrender these items at the time the sheriff serves this Order on you. If the weapons cannot be surrendered at that time, you must surrender them to the sheriff within 24 hours at the time and place specified by the sheriff. Failure to surrender the weapons and permits as ordered or possessing, owning, purchasing, or receiving a firearm, ammunition or permits to purchase or carry concealed firearms after being ordered not to possess firearms, ammunition or permits is a crime. See "Notice To Parties," To The Defendant," on Page 4 of this Order for information regarding the penalty for these crimes and instructions on how to request retrieval of surrendered weapons when the protective order is no longer in effect.

- [ ] 14. the defendant shall attend and complete an abuser treatment program offered by the following agency, which is approved by the Domestic Violence Commission: [08]

AOC-CV-306, Page 3 of 4, Rev. 3/04
© 2004 Administrative Office of the Courts

(Over)

STATE OF NORTH CAROLINA

Wake County

File No. ___ CV

In The General Court Of Justice
District Court Division

Name Of Plaintiff

_____
VERSUS
Name And Address Of Defendant

MOTION ☑ TO RENEW ☐ OR SET ASIDE
**DOMESTIC VIOLENCE
PROTECTIVE ORDER
NOTICE OF HEARING**

G.S. 50B 3(b)

MOTION

A Domestic Violence Protective Order, a copy of which is attached, was entered by a district court judge in this county on the date listed below and has an expiration date as listed below. *(Attach a copy of the order.)*

☑ 1. I move that the Domestic Violence Protective Order previously entered on the date listed below and not yet expired be renewed for an additional year and request the court to set a hearing date to determine whether the order will be renewed. *(State facts that cause you to want to renew the order, including new acts of violence, if any; violations of the order, if any; and give any other reasons you believe the order should be renewed.)*

☐ 2. I move that the Domestic Violence Protective Order previously entered on the date listed below be set aside because it is no longer equitable that the order have future application or for other good cause pursuant to G.S. 1A-1, Rule 60(b)(5) or (6), and I request the Court to set a hearing date to determine whether the order will be set aside ☐ and if it is set aside, whether a new protective order will be entered. *(State reasons for setting aside protective order.)*

Date Previous Order Entered: Aug 5 2004
Date Of Expiration Of Previous Order: Aug 5 2005

Date: _____
Signature Of Plaintiff/Defendant

NOTICE OF HEARING

NOTICE TO THE PARTIES: You are hereby notified that this Motion To ☐ Renew ☐ Set Aside the Domestic Violence Protective Order will be heard on the date, time and at the location set out below. You should appear at that time to show cause, if any, why the relief requested in this Motion should not be allowed.

Date Of Hearing: 8 3 05
Time Of Hearing: 9 ☐ AM ☐ PM
Location Of Hearing: 90

CERTIFICATE OF SERVICE

I certify that on the date of mailing shown below a copy of this Motion and Notice was served on the defendant/plaintiff at the address listed above by depositing a copy in a post-paid, properly addressed envelope in a post office or official depository under the exclusive care and custody of the United States Postal Service.

Date Of Mailing | Date Of Certification | Signature Of Plaintiff/Defendant

AOC-CV-313, Rev. 11/03
© 2003 Administrative Office of the Courts
(See INSTRUCTIONS on Reverse)
Original-File Copy Defendant Copy-Plaintiff

To:	Anderson	**From:**	J'Anmetra
Fax:		**Pages:**	1
Phone:		**Date:**	8/4/2005
Re:	Case	**CC:**	

X Urgent ☐ For Review ☐ Please Comment ☐ Please Reply ☐ Please Recycle

● **Comments:**

Good morning,

Thank you for calling me back on yesterday. However, when I went to court on the 3rd for the continuous of the restraining order, the judge decided to have everything to be heard at one time on August the 10th. So I would still need representation for the dismissal, and child custody. Mr. lawyer is still planning on being dismissed from the case. I would really appreciate some legal representation on my part so that I may know exactly what is going. I know I have been in contact with everyone in the office, and they have been very helpful. I am just seeking some additional help so that I can put all of this behind me. If after you receive this information and your office feels they still may not be of any service to me, please contact me so that I may prepare my self for court on the 10th.

Thank you again for all of your help and advice.

J'Anmetra L.

Fax

To:	Amy	**From:**	J'Anmetra
Fax:		**Pages:**	1
Phone:		**Date:**	8/10/2005
Re:	Questions	**CC**	Anderson

X Urgent   ☐ For Review   ☐ Please Comment   ☐ Please Reply   ☐ Please Recycle

● **Comments:**

Good afternoon,

I just wanted to give an update for my case. I was in court to day for the extension of the Domestic Violence order and my husband's motion to dismiss. However, he dropped the motion to dismiss and I was granted my restraining order for another year. Now I have another problem and that would be child custody. I would appreciate any legal assistance that is available to me and I am not sure if this organization takes on cases for Child Custody. I called the Clerk's Office and they informed that I could not file the forms myself but that I need an attorney to do that. Please advise, I am doing a Calendar Request for August 29th with Judge Green. I went to that office this morning and the front desk assistant gave me that information.

Tuesday, August 09, 2005

Opening Statement

Reason for Extension of Restraining Order

I am here today to get an extension on the restraining order against Mr. _____ because I am still afraid that he may try to kill me.
- Examples of times trying to kill you
- What he promised if you ever took his child
- What he promised to tell the court and police
- If he was brave enough to come to the house and put a note on the door next he will try and come through the door
- He promised me that he would make me pay some way somehow because he believes I stole his mothers money…and I believe he intends to do just that
- Raped me last time I was with him, tried to have me committed to a mental hospital.
- Told church I had emotional problems…lied to his family and friends
- Had me reported missing – missing persons report in Fayetteville, NC.
- Bought a new car. So I would not know if he was following me.
- Officer _____ has the original copy of what was left on the door from my 911 call.
- 2 911 calls made 1st to report note; 2nd because I thought Mr. _____ was outside the door
- Mr. _____ also lied about his date of birth when arrested court record shows 4-16/1_____ DOB is _____
- Mr. _____ pleaded guilty to violating restraining order on August 3, 2005
- On July 27, 2004 Mr. _____ took all of the money out of the checking and savings account and had them transferred into another account in his name (I have the account number)

Separated July 25th, 2004 6:11am –
1st time contacted anyone by email Aug 10th → Bishop

I don't think this need to be dismissed out of court. The paper to my understanding says "30 days to respond in writing" which he day however, he had 10 days to appear in court. Served on august 3, Deputy _____, Victim Services Unit of Wake County, court date was August 5, 2005.
- Mr. _____ claims there was a funeral he had to attend according to all local papers, church secretary of _____ AME Zion Church in Clarkton, there was no funeral
- Mr. _____ had not reported to his pulpit, Presiding Elder Florence _____, or Bishop _____, or the new Bishop _____, that is why Presiding Elder took over the church because Mr. _____ had not contacted anyone until Aug 15, 2005
- 3 separate occasions Fayetteville police went to Bent Pine Drive and he did not answer, the church sent them out to check on him, on the 3rd visit he answered.

- At Duke University Hospital, the nurse asked me if I was in danger, Mr. told me he wished I would have bleed to death so that he would not have to deal with.
- He would not allow me to breast feed daughter because he didn't want me to become attached to her. because I had to train his new wife and she would take care of child
- I wasn't allowed to sleep.
- I went to work immediately after giving birth. even though the doctor had me on complete bed rest because I refused a blood transfusion
- I was completely cut off from my family

QUESTIONS

1. Location and date of funeral
2. How did Mr.   find out where I was living
3. At Church in Charlotte – Smith dictates... why did you tear up Church after getting assault & your ex-wife was asked to stay with you? Had she already left?

Closing

I have seen Mr.   go from sweet and loving to out right rage ...throwing things.threatneing to hit if you answer the question in correctly
- I was told when to go to the bathroom and how to go
- When to eat
- He had control of all money, phone.
- I was not allowed to talk to daughter, play with her
- She was not allowed out side
- Mr.   looked at teenage pornography on line

MR. _____

Cell: 919
@netzero.com

March 17, 2005

Dear J'anmetra,

I hope this letter finds you and the rest of the _____ family under the richest blessings of God!

I am writing you to bring you up to speed on several issues that concern you and the at least one of the children. I was recently in the hospital with pancreatitis, blood pressure, and heart problems. It is amazing how fast an older person can have their health go south when they loose all the people in their life in one hour and never hear from them again (especially a 3 1/2 month old newborn) all the hospital personnel could not believe that after all the burdens from your past that I was forced to bear that anybody could be so cruel. If I go into a coma, who would be there to carry out my wishes. They thought they were going to have to do emergency surgery, but were hesitant to do so without my spouse present or at least accessible to them by phone pager or something.

That is okay because all of that has been forgiven. How easy was it to forgive yourself but not me? Who is being daddy or uncle to _____ now, like I was for _____ even thought I was fool enough to believe you rather than _____ and his wife and you are now doing the same thing to me. Jo, has it ever struck you that you are doing exactly what you said you despised in your mother? How she ditched you and your sister to move on to the next man, who would always be better than the last.

And what about the rights of _____ and _____? Jo, how confused are you making those children by exposing them to people that have Christian children going to a Muslim school. That's who you're following?

Jo, like me you have an emotional disorder that does not have to destroy you, your children, or your marriage. However, it is necessary for you to stop running and just get the help that you need, as I have.

Jo, loving someone is a real adult responsibility, so is parenting. Some people really do know how to love through mistakes especially those they cause for others.

I want to share something with you that was shared with me some few weeks ago in a convention in Raleigh. There was a Catholic Nun who was in recovery 23 years, she said that every time she spoke she prayed with and for the people to whom she spoke and did it for the rest of her life. This was her prayer: <u>"I PRAY THAT EACH OF YOU ON THE DAY OF YOUR DEATH, WILL BE WHAT GOD MEANT YOU TO BE ON THE DAY OF YOUR BIRTH!"</u> It left us all in tears, all 630 of us could not leave that place without touching her. I told her of the guilt and shame that I had suffered from losing my ministry, wife, children, home and all my worldly goods and all of my faith. She told me that all of us who share the relationship with God of clergy carry a special guilt and shame, but not to let others hold us more responsible than they hold themselves.

I now live in my car. I have to job. I have no money. I remember that I was always there for you and   when you were sick and in trouble even if I did get mad. I NEVER LEFT YOUR SIDE GOOD DAYS OR BAD! What responsibility do you have now to me? I feel you feel none cause God   told you so. Even they took from me Jo. And you allowed it. I guess when you judge a preacher to be bad with all of your arrogance then y'all know best.

I wonder what God will say when looks at y'alls track record. I gave money to all of you. Do any of you owe it back to me? I helped all of you one way or another, but none of you owe the bad man anything do you.

          cannot be another victim of what you were told was okay. Jo' you do have a choice. How dare you complain to me about how your family did you, but now you have justification to do it to   and   ? I am I that bad of a father or husband, or was this just what you planned all along.

I have learned that life and health is very fragile. You should know that better than most. I want another chance with you and the girls. I deserve one just for giving more than you did <u>every last thing I had. And you know this.</u> I need you to call me. I want to see the kids before their birthdays. It's been 8 months. I have suffered in silence up to now. However, I need something from you now. You can share this with you and your self righteous friends and have a good laugh, or you can step up to the plate, which is all that you were ever ask to do.

Jo, you ask me if you could not have a child would I still want to marry you? Do you remember my answer? Let me ask you a question. Since I am old have made some mistakes in our marriage, since I am no longer employed, since I don't have a job, since I gave more than I ever got, since I am no longer a pastor or minister, can you love and give to me what I gave to you? A home, hope, forgiveness, loyalty, gentleness, or even tough love?

I am sick and even considering a disability. Something which I thought I would never do. Call me, please.

One thing Jo. Did you really think leaving everything was going to make up for what you had taken? The greatest gift we all have, *time and our health.* Even leaving them was a selfish act.   and   have not even told Mom & Dad   cause they all loved you and   as they loved me for all of my life.   ried with me and for me.   was shocked and hurt.   and   are willing to do anything they can to get us back together and serve as mediators for both of us because they have seen my pain.

Guess what. I am so relieved to not be pursuing the ministry any more. It was never in my temperament. So you don't have to worry about being a ministers wife any more. I want to go back to school to become a nurse. Loosing everything has made me more humble and that was necessary. For God to use me the way he wanted to outside the ministry.

I have been to church on three occasion since you left. I have a hard time being where so much harm has been dome to me. I hope you have taken the time and effort to get   the help she needs with having felt it necessary to tell someone that she had been molested.

If God has forgiven you for putting her in that kid of environment, then maybe you owe me and him a chance for our marriage to be sacred and blessed. Have you done the work?

You have been given the gift of time by me. Time to heal, time to grow. If I can give you eight months and take the pain of this separation maybe you can give me a call, what could be the harm? All you have to do is hang up.

Please consider what has been said to you in this letter. Pray and ask God for the strength and courage to confront your past with your husband that did not start as he ended. The pain you inflicted on me was devastating. Did you not even care enough to at least call after all this time to say hello? You at least did that for   and   .

This is my prayer for our family: I pray that our motives for having our children and harming each other are not the same today as they were 8 months ago. I pray that God has spoken to your heart as he did mine that you might receive wisdom and courage for both of us to right our wrong in the sight of God and in the interest of our children. I pray that we will both never speak of our past together or before except the good days of laughter we spent together. I pray that our loyalty to each other will be greater than to our friends and that God will forgive us both and lead us to him in truth. My number and email is listed on this letter. I live in Raleigh if only to be close to all of you.

New rules:

- You handle your family, I want nothing to do with them.
- I want   to have nothing to do with them because how they sought to destroy what God hath joined together.
- We never speak of our past relationship or your past or mine.
- Everybody does their own banking everything is 50/50.
- Nobody swears or is aggressive.
- We have separate friend as long as they don't threaten our relationship
- Nobody yells
- Nobody thinks totally of themselves and what they can get from the other with no plan to help and honor each others rights
- Everybody is honest and has no hidden agendas.
-          and his wife get to see
- Our kids come first
- Everybody goes to counseling when they have a problem that they cannot solve themselves
- We share the debts that have been just left on me Jo, (that's fair).
- We love each other and never go to bed without telling each other that and kissing before we say goodnight or leave the house.
- We both apologize to each other and mean it and don't do it anymore.

If you have some or are not with someone new which you may be. You can add or change them. Jo, I told   and .   that if you had been in a relationship with someone else all bets were off. What do you think?

I hope if nothing else you have not made that kid of mistake with   that you did with   . But if so let us work it out now.

All my love,

Your Husband,

PS

I guess your response to this note will really speak to who you are and what you really wanted three years ago won't it? I hope you love me as much as you said in your diary. You know I never knew that you felt the way you described in your diary. That is evidence, of a great love. However, it does not match what you said in counseling to me or Mrs.   . I don't know what to believe as usual.

Feel free to have me arrested
If you choose

www.ingramcontent.com/pod-product-compliance
Lightning Source LLC
Chambersburg PA
CBHW071522080526
44588CB00011B/1529